To be 17 again, or maybe re-think that,

Even before reaching 17 in January in the fi[...] beautiful place in the world that is the north [...] Ireland, in her young, tormented and sad hea[...] ...[wors]t and cruellest of environments to be in. It had always been a sad, loud, busy, confusing, stress filled, abusive, horrible existence and hard filled time to just to survive childhood, and now to even make it to 17 years old was a battle in itself for a young wan that was losing the will to carry on because her very soul had been repeatedly taken from her physically and mentally and destroyed in so many different ways through the years of her younger life, and now as she reaches 17, she works to provide for her mum and young sister while attending her last 6 months of school and yet little does she know, but she is also a couple of weeks into a heart breaking pregnancy too at the time just before meeting the very first and as she thought back then the forever true love of her life.

From the outside everyone thought it was a very privileged life for her, Growing up in the Inisfail hotel in Lisdoonvarna, A Dad, a Mum and with a new baby sister after 7 years of being an only child. Wanting for nothing, Best of clothes, Best of toys, Best of everything given to her but the reality was very different in her young life. What she wanted and needed the most was never bestowed to her. In a village where the tourist season was always from Easter to October in this little village with its 2 schools, 3 shops and 14 hotels and pubs in the summer but only 3 pubs open throughout the winter. You worked hard during the season and school was often missed as you were required and expected to get stuck in and carry on with no complaint or negotiation as this was your expectation since you were 6 years old, If you can walk, talk and carry something you had a job and get on with it. And when she was 7 she was handed a new baby sister to take care of as well.

Her parents were all for putting on a show of being better off then they actually were. The father wanted to always come across as the good husband, great Dad and successful business man and the pioneer who had never touched alcohol which made him some sort of saint in some peoples eyes. And yes, it was easy to hold up his image as the pub of the hotel was always busy with people but only because as the tills were taking in the money he was lending it back out to anyone that asked for a loan just to have it said that it was a busy pub. The mother always came across as the glamour of the establishment as she gave hours putting on her perfect face, styling her hair, with the finest expensive jewellery on her with her high end jeans and heels that defied gravity, He kept the customers happy with the repeated loans and she kept them happy with the view, banter and flirting and sitting outside the counter at night to drink with customers which of course would always lead to numerous arguments between the two of them which meant they had one of the most disruptive, argumentative, jealousy driven and toxic relationships that was ever between two people. It was not a family life, it was torture, there were no holidays, no meals together, no snuggles, no praise when she done good but plenty of punishment when she was bad and in their eyes she was bad and trouble all the time. She was 7 now and worked as hard as any adult in the hotel. No breaks for her, no days out with cousins, or playing with friends, nothing that resembled a childhood was bestowed on her. Hard work and abuse were her normality. She was always the very best that she could be but somehow she was always in trouble and waiting on her next punishment. Her Father and mothers prime role was hoteliers, Secondary role was as parents, Money was the most important thing and their daughters were just there to be paraded in their finery and want of nothing. Every season was filled with hard work, little rest or sleep, and just pitch in wherever needed from early 7am until 2am or 3am the following morning, and just do it with no complaint or she would be dealt with. Her parents always borrowed heavily from their bank in the winter to keep up their lavish lifestyle of the summer and throughout the summer the work was relentless in order to pay back those loans every year. There was no business sense to it, Just borrow from the bank and then pay back every season. There was also an ever going roundabout of staff that would arrive from all parts of the country willing to work for their bed, board and wage as Lisdoonvarna was the place to for the craic back then and it was a right of passage for plenty of young people to go to Lisdoonvarna for seasonal work, but come Monday morning they would be for the sack and a whole new bunch of workers were brought in and only a very select, reliable and trusted few were kept. You worked hard and you were under Mary's management and temper. Mary the mother was the glamour, the self indulged, the tormentor, the prime boss and abrupt and ignorant with anyone that needed putting in their place, Peter was the Father that was the pioneer, the one that wanted the approval of everyone so came across as the quieter, hard done by husband, who would play the victim when they argued and lock himself in a bedroom with a bottle of whiskey to convince the tormented child that he would drink it because the mother was giving out to him and the child would scream outside the locked door for her Daddy not to drink it because he would die. Always a game with them but there was never a winner in any of these games and situations, only suffering and heart break for a child that craved peace and love.

Money, possessions or clothes was never any use to the older girl, she craved a family, a peace, a hug, a parents kiss, a sense of security, a knowing that she was safe, a feeling of being ok, But instead it was a life behind closed doors of regular beatings, humiliations, abuse and violence towards a child that often prayed to God to die while she lay there in a pool of her own blood, tasting it and trying to cough it up to get it up her throat because she was nauseous from swallowing it. Even attempting to cough took every bit of her being to do as she lay there confused, in pain, bewildered, wondering how long she was there, wanting to die, wanting to disappear, wanting it to stop. She didn't feel able to take any more, broken bones, nose bleeds, busted lips and broken bleeding wounds received from her fathers belt, his punches, his kicks while her mother held her down to receive the beatings that she so deserved as she pleaded and begged of her to please let her go and she wouldn't do anything to make them mad ever again. The beatings that were bestowed upon her young body just because she was there and there was no consequence or punishment to them and somehow it was acceptable because she was bold, she was ugly, she was stupid, she was fat, she was in the way, she was a waste of space, she was nothing and she did not matter, and she had to be reminded regularly how horrible she was in case she ever forgot. Why did she have to be there, Was this her only purpose, Was this how it was always going to be, She just accepted it as she knew no better and her will had been beaten out of her for many years before as she had received many slaps on the face for crying when she would fall or be upset, to cry was unacceptable to them. Her cousin has recounted to her how her mother and father had visited her family one time and she was only around 3 years old and so while the adults were in the pub her cousin baby sat the 2 year old and was asleep on the couch when they got back from the pub. The child woke up with the noise of them back and started to cry and received a slap across the face for crying as she had been woken up by them. Her cousin took the toddler to her room to sleep as her cousin was shocked as how easily and quickly the slap had taken place and how now quite the toddler was. Always put down, always put in her place, always stay quite, always in trouble for something. As she got older she would think that maybe they would be happier if she was gone, It would be easier for everyone if she wasn't here, and as she grew older the abuse got more regular and more violent. She often spent her days and nights in a bedroom with numerous, painful injuries trying to recover as best she could, Needing time to heal on her body and her mind and trying to understand why. When she was able to function somewhat, to need food, to need a drink, to dress herself without the pain, to cope without crying, when her swollen face had gone down, when the black eyes had gone down, when she could walk without any reminder to them about what had happened it was then OK to come back down to be amongst other people while they looked at her empathically and with tears in their eyes at her because they knew that if they reached out to her to console her it would be her that was punished all over again. She couldn't draw attention to her and her injuries. She would just get food and a drink and sit silently having it and feeling so lost, so upset, so tired, so ashamed and so unloved and yet hold a steady hand and don't cry because someone will reach out to help you and if they did she would feel the wrath of her parents again. To save her, the people around her had to try and ignore what was happening just to keep her safe from another horrendous episode. The kindest thing to do was to leave her be, to her feeling the shame and humiliation that was hers alone to deal with because she deserved it. Nobody could help or interfere, it was safer for her to be left alone. Some adults did sneak a kind word, a knowing glance, a sad look at her but never too near, It might be fatal some day to help her. Her only care that time was her now little 2 year old sister who had the instinct to be quite and to just be in the room with her because her little mind knew that her big sister was sad and that little baby girl gave her strength when she needed it because she now had a growing fear that her little sister would be treated to the same outbursts when she got older so her will now was to survive and protect her from what was her sickening normality. They often spent hours in that room, the baby sister would be playing with toys and the older sister while minding the little one was put ironing sheets and pillowcases in a rotary iron for hours on end when she was able but not ready to be seen by anyone else as her face was too battered and emotional to be seen in public.

For her continued time as one of the privileged children in the hotel her life was getting harder to cope with. She was the full-time care taker of her little sister, the extra staff member when required, often working until 3 in the morning and up again at 7 to serve breakfast to guests before going to school, Her welcomed break sometimes, where she would occasionally fall asleep at her desk and receive several knocks on the back of the head to wake up and concentrate in class or other knocks and slaps because there was no homework done or mass was not attended on the Sunday because there was work to be done in the hotel, and so even at school she was humiliated, scorned and punished. Evry envoirment She craved the visits from cousins from Dublin who would be visiting for a few weeks at a time and they would be staying in a mobile home in Fanore and she sometimes would get to go on a little holiday to Fanore for a couple of nights with them but there was also times that excuses were made as to why she couldn't go because she was black and blue from beatings and it was her fault that she couldn't go because if she wasn't such a torment she wouldn't have had to have been dealt with. But she had 2 wonderful men that did visit from Dublin. Pj and Andy were 1st cousins of her fathers and when they arrived with their children for a few days holiday they took her out everyday for drives, for fishing, for sightseeing, for ice cream and they gave the bestest hugs ever, She always felt secure, and loved and safe with them and still today has a great love for both of them. She was allowed go with them as there was no swimming so no reason to tog out and no suspicions raised. They were aware that she had a hard time with her parents, and working and taking care of her little sister and had spoken to the parents to let her live a little so against their will they let her have a break with Pj and Andy because those 2 men would have torn them both apart if they knew the full extent of the truth and how bad the situation really was. She continued and coped as best she could but as she grew older it was becoming more humiliating and shameful to be her. Puberty was starting and somehow to her parents they thought it was disgusting, ugly and horrendous thing to be happening and now she was a whore as well because of the changes that were occurring to her. She would be reminded of this every time she was dragged into their bedroom, begging to not do it, begging them to stop, begging them that whatever she had done wrong she would never do it again, just begging PLEASE. These beatings took a different turn as she was growing, They became more violent, more severe, more humiliating and more regular. At least once a week was the regular amount of times but sometimes there were more episodes. Sometimes she would be dragged by her long hair to the bedroom for the beatings, Other times she was just called for and would just present herself in the room and as soon as she woud walk into that room she was pounced upon, usually a punch to the face to knock her to the bed. She had become robotic to it. She could be in any part of the hotel but once she heard her mother roaring that her father wanted her she woud just automatically make her way upstairs where they were waiting with fire and temper in their eyes, almost like crazed wild wolves snarling at their prey ready to attack and kill. She surrendered to her fate as it was all she knew and there is nobody to help her or take her away from it. She would plead not to be tied up as usual because as she got older the restraints tied on her legs and arms got tighter to stop her protecting herself from the lashings on her naked growing body, because now all her clothing and underwear was being ripped and torn off her, and as she twisted and turned with every lash of his belt or their fists, the punches, the kicking's, the slaps and the roaring words of how disgusting and dirty she was, it was the humiliation of her being naked that was somehow more hurting to her than the physical pain. There was no more a reason for it, there was no explanation for it, There was nothing only acceptance for it. This is the way it is and nobody will save her. She is just a 12 year old dirty whore that deserves it. All she craved was someone to love her.

The one person whose love she was sure of was her little sister who by now had started school and it was her responsibility to have her ready each day and bring her to school with her and on her break at 2 o clock bring her sister home and drop her off in home before returning to school herself for her final hour.

In 1984, she was 11 and it was the summer holidays from school. When her parents and the little sister would go to the cash and carry suppliers in Ennis she was left at home in the hotel to keep an eye on things while they were away for those hours. She would keep track of how many were in for food or in the bar or checked in to stay. As usual there was and endless turnover of staff but theire was also a few that were a constant there. One of the full time staff was a thirty odd year old man that came from Limerick to work for them in the hotel and he was a loner and kept very much to himself and got on with his work. He returned in 1985 for another season and he was left to get on with his work as he knew from the year before. She didn't have much interaction with him but he was nice to her and kind when needs be. Just by saying hello to her made her feel that she wasn't invisible and that was nice at the time. It became a kind of secret that he was saying hello and asking how she was. He started to touch her hand, touch her arm as he passed. It was alien to her and she was just as confused as to why anyone would be nice to her. This eventually led to him meeting her in the hallway, on corridors, at the back of the bar where he would ask her for a hug, which she freely gave as she craved a hug so badly. This led to kissing, and then onto her fondling him where he wanted by being guided by him in every move. She knew there was something wrong and dirty about it. To him and others it was abuse of that 12 year old girl, But to her it was confusing because he must care about her to be so nice to her and she must be nice back. This continued for about 2 months, maybe once a week when her parents were away at the cash and carry. It was a secret to be kept by her as he had told her that she would be taken away if anyone ever found out about it. He was caught one day, Thankfully, and all hell completely broke out. Upon her parents return from a cash and carry trip it finally stopped. They had arrived back early and caught him with her and immediately were aware that something was going on but not sure of the scale of what was going on. To her there was nothing wrong because he didn't hurt her, he didn't criticise her, he didn't make her feel like nothing, He was nice to her and that was all she needed. The shouting started, The blame started, the threat of police started. if he didn't leave right now. He packed his bags, He left that day and she was left in a world of confusion and fear and in no doubt what was coming to her. The doctor was summoned for an examination and a pregnancy test which was not required as there was never any sex between them but the parents were convinced she was a whore and brought it on herself and she will suffer for her mistake with him. She was to blame and she brought it on herself, Sure what else was to be expected from her.

The doctor arrived, a nice man, he was the family doctor for all of them since they had arrived in Lisdoonvarna, but given the circumstances he should have also called a social worker but it wasn't his place to apparently or his care for what was going on. The doctor left after the test and she knew that she would possibly die that evening because of what was coming to her. She had no where to escape to she had to stay and take her punishment. It didn't take long to be summoned for her fate, She pleaded with all that she had not to have to do it, she swore she was so sorry for the way she was, she begged to them let go, to stop dragging, kicking and punching her up the stairs, She already had received untold injuries from downstairs from them to now be in the room stripped naked with hands and legs tied and a gag on her to dull the screaming with each blow and punch and kick and stomach gurgling blow that she received. The whore would be dealt with and that was that. With each blow she received she did scream into her gag with the pain of each strike as it hit her, It felt like there was not one inch of her body or face left untouched by this particular episode on that day. This was the day she would die.

She wasn't sure what day or time it was when she awoke on her bed, having dragged and dumped on her bed, Naked, Cold, In pain, Blood everywhere, barely able to open her eyes, tasting her blood, Chunks of her hair around her but still here, it was the pain that told her she was alive. Why couldn't she just die. Can't even do that right and not be such a burden on everyone. It would be an end to this life and she would have peace and so would they so they would be happy. Again the now five year old little sister came in with a bottle of orange juice from the bar for her that she had sneaked upstairs in case she was caught, and gave her a little hug and ran back out as quick in case she was found upstairs with her. Sometimes she thinks that those little moments might have been the ones that saved her. It took her quite a few days to recover, one of her parents would come in sometimes just to throw a sandwich, a drink or a dinner on the dressing table but she was not able to move or eat for a number of days. Things soon went back to the normal regular abuse but of course the extra element now was that she was now a true whore like they knew all along and she was set for nothing else in life only to be a dirty slut and whore and a burden to them forever with her disgrace and carry on. She would result to nothing in life. And in case she forgot she was reminded everyday what a burden she was. After another bad beating and in desperation she managed to escape out the front door one day after a beating, badly injured and barely able to walk when she met the local priest who asked what happened to her and she told him her mother and father had beaten her, she thought maybe he would help her, instead he dragged her back to the hotel and told her parents to keep their business indoors and not on the streets. She got another beating as punishment for upsetting the priest.

Her life continued on like this while she started the next part of it with the beginning of secondary school in 1985, She settled in well and liked this more grown up system and break from home. She wasn't part of the popular group but she fitted in as best as she could and done the best she could to get by and cope as best she could with the next chapter of her life. She enjoyed school and did well in class and done well in exams and tests. She didn't miss as much school because the secondary school were stricter on school days missed which suited her fine. In May that year her little sister had an accident at the hotel.

There was a bus load of people booked in for lunch and so she was off school that day to help. The then 5 year old sister was put in the pantry up from the hotel kitchen to do some painting with her colouring book and paints so as not to get in the way while everyone was so busy with the bus loads of visitors. The pantry was were the washing of the dishes took place with a big catering dishwasher and two large sinks also for washing pots and pans. The man that was responsible for that area had run a deep sink full of hot water to leave things soaking as he received them while the rush was on with the lunch service. Everyone had their position and everyone was busy when an almighty scream could be heard throughout the kitchen and dining room. Straight away she knew there was something terribly wrong with the little sister. She ran to her to find her balancing herself over a sink as the stool that she had used to climb up onto to reach the taps to change her dirty water for clean water for her painting pictures had slipped out from under her and she now had her arm and chest in the boiling hot water in the sink. From the pitching scream everyone knew that she was scalded. As she was lifted off the sink the steam just rose off her and she was in horrendous pain and torture and bless her she was in screaming with the pain. For no good reason the child was dressed with mutiple layers that day, she even had a wool Aran sweater which soaked up the boiling water and held the heat on her. She was hysterical and her clothes were being removed but as the clothes came off her skin from her arm and chest also came with them. She was doing all she could to calm her, Someone was on the phone to the emergency department in the hospital 25 miles away and the advice was to wrap her in a cold, wet, white sheet and get her to the hospital immediately. It was decided that the mother would stay at the hotel and so the father and the older sister had to go to the hospital with the child. There were steps leading onto a lane way at the side of the pantry and there was a very heavy downpour of rain at that moment and her sister just went out into it and stood in it as she seemed to be getting relief from the cold rain. Their father raced at brake neck speed to the hospital while she had her little sister in her arms wrapped in the wet white sheet. The little one had gone into shock as she was just staring straight ahead and all colour had left her face. She was unresponsive to talk from her father or her sister. There was a huge urgency to get her to the emergency department as the silence from her was deafening and hugely worrying as she had been screaming in agony but now there was no response from her only little short quick breaths. She was brought in straight away and she was in a bad way with very blisters that had formed on her arm and chest. They intermediately had an iv in each food as her hands and arms were burnt but her left arm was a lot worse. She just lay there oblivious to the 2 doctors and nurses working on her and treating her burns. They sedated her and gave pain relief which was a great relief to the child. The mother had now arrived but both her and the father were not physically able to stay by the little girl because they were so nauseous looking at the burns on her body. Her older sister was able to stay by her as it didn't affect her looking at the burns, She wanted to stay with her anyway regardless of how hard it was to watch while they treated her. The parents waited in the waiting room only coming in when summoned about vaccinations, questions about how it happened and forms to be filled in and signed. After many hours the little one was stable but still sedated because of the level of pain she would be in if fully awake. It was now night and it was time for everyone to leave except one person to stay with her. The parents were to go home as they couldn't watch or stomach when the burns were exposed for treatment or dressing and so the older sister stayed to comfort and take care of the younger sister. They went and got food and drinks for her and they would see her tomorrow. The little one was being taken out of sedation more and more during the night and receiving painkillers through the iv but as the night went on she was more uncomfortable with pain and afraid in the hospital and of the doctors and nurses hurting her every time they checked the burns or had to dress them. The following day arrived and the parents landed to see them. The older girl was brought out for some breakfast while the other parent stayed with the injured child. There was magazines bought for them both, sweets, drinks, a doll for the younger one and a Sony Walkman for the older girl with a Wham cassette to play as they were her favourite band at the time, It made it a little easier to stay in the hospital but looking back she feels that they would have bought anything once they didn't have to stay in the hospital or look at those raw burns. They would leave the room anytime the burns had to be checked or new dressings applied. Before they would go home in the evening they would again get food for the older girl and promises of being back tomorrow to see them both. This routine continued for 5 nights and six days. It was extremely hard on both girls as the little one was admitted to a ward that had three very old people in it and the little one was terrified of them because it is possible that these old people were a bit disorientated themselves as they slept a lot during the day but would be raving and shouting a lot at night so it was very uncomfortable and a bit scary for both girls to be in that ward. The little one would beg to go home and the older one was exhausted as her bed was an armchair. On the 6th day something snapped with her parents as they were going to discharge the young girl and arrangements were made for daily trips back to the hospital for the dressings to be changed. The little sister was still in a huge amount of pain and the older girl was exhausted from staying in the hospital by her sisters side. They got home and the care of the little was solely down to the older girl. Taking care of her every need and responsible for anything that was required by her and this included going to the hospital everyday and staying with her while her bandages were changed and trying to soothe her through it as it was a gruelling and traumatic experience every time. After a couple of weeks this was a every second day trip and eventually it was the district nurse that would call to treat and dress the burns at the hotel. School was missed for the remainder of the term for the little one and the remainder of the older girls school term was sporadic as she was needed home to look after the little girl. Thankfully she healed well and after a couple of months was back to herself and everything was back to normality for everyone. Work, childminding, and her episodes of being the thing for her parents to take their anger and frustration out on. It was getting more sinister and violent and was taking an element pure shame on her. She was now a well developed girl as puberty has started the year before and it was with shame and humiliation that she was experiencing as she was beaten and commented on about her body as they beat down on her with full force and temper. To her it was embarrassing, humiliating and shameful that they were seeing her developing body, beating her body and then telling her how ugly and disgusting she was. Her head was being destroyed now as well as her body but with strength from somewhere she was holding on as best she could.

Things between her parents were starting to get rocky. They had always had a tempestuous relationship. She had asked her mother how they met and how they started going out with each other as he was from Fernhill, Lisdoonvarna in Co. Clare, and she was from Timahoe, Co. Kildare. They were both working in Dublin when they met. The mother had left her home at 12 years old to work with her older sister in Jervis Street hospital in Dublin. Back then when you were finished national school you could leave school and go to work. When they were younger they would work in Bord Na Mona footing turf and their mother would collect their wages. When the mothers older sister was 14 she left to go and work for the nuns in Dublin at the hospital and she would send home some of her wages to help the household in Kildare. Her mother desperately wanted to join her older sister in Dublin so when they were on a visit to Dublin to visit the sister she boldly asked the nun if their was any job for her. The nun took it into consideration and as her older sister ws such a great worker and they were sisters the nun gave her a job. She moved to Dublin and accommodation and food was included in the job with a good enough wage included. It suited her perfectly. She was good with money and was able to save a little and send money home to her mother every week as well. She loved Dublin, she worked hard and was working her way up in the nuns esteem and eventually was training to work on the switchboard in the hospital. After her training she got a full time job on the switchboard and much better pay. She had been there now for 5 years in Dublin and was loving her life there. She enjoyed her social nights too and one night she met a man from Co. Clare that was a barman in Madigans pub in Dublin. They had met at a dance and got on well. He done all the chasing and she said he was a little stalker-ish in his actions. He was putting a lot more effort into the courtship than her but they got on with it. They were together for a time and he asked her to marry him and she agreed as he said he couldn't cope if she refused and said he would throw himself under a bus if it was a no. She said yes, and so began a relationship and marriage that in my opinion should never have happened. They got married soon after and decided to move to London and he got a job as a barman and she had a job in Guy's hospital helping nurses to take care of premature and sick babies. She loved her job but missed Ireland. She did get pregnant while there but lost the baby sometime into the pregnancy. She went back to work and sometime later she was pregnant again. They decided to move back to Dublin in 1972 and he got a job back in Madigans as a barman while she was pregnant and she was getting ready for the new baby soon after in January. Their first living child arrived on January 6th 1973 and all was well. They got on with their life as a new family and it was all going well but soon enough Dublin was in bother in 1974 with bombings that were happening and the mother was afraid to live there any more. They moved down to her home place in Kildare where her aunt had a house and they stayed there for 6 months until they took the decision to move to his home place in Clare. He took a job in his brothers hotel in Lisdoonvarna called the Bellview and they were staying with his brother and his family in the hotel. During this time another hotel in the square in Lisdoonvarna came up for sale and the parents decided to go after it and buy it for themselves. They were successful in the purchase and so a new chapter began in Lisdoonvarna in 1975. They had no experience but threw themselves into their new life and being busy suited them as they didn't need to spend time together and the baba was a great distraction but their one commonality. He was always suspicious of his wife and always keeping an eye on her and her movements, who she was talking to, interacting with and listening to conversations that she would be having. She was suspicious of him as he was always disappearing for a time and wouldn't appear until every nook, cranny and rooms were explored but yet no sign of him. He would always claim that he was at the shop or at his friends house for a minute or on the street talking to someone or somewhere in the hotel fixing something. She could never figure out where he was and it infuriated her but he always convinced her that he was innocent in everything. These disappearing acts wouldn't come to light until a some years later. Around that time video players came around and one was got for the bar but it was a pure nuisance as far as the mother was concerned as the father was spending most of his nights in the bar when it was closed to watch porn videos which she would confront him about and he would again deny all knowledge even though the mother would opening catch him in the bar watching them and her response was always to physically remove the video player from the shelf and smash it off the floor. It was an obsession with him and a few of his local friends that would swap these videos amongst themselves and it was filling her with temper that this was going on. He would be up most of the nights saying he was more or less keeping an eye on everything but he was actually up to no good. And again he was mad for the latest gadgets as she thought when he then bought a Poloraid carmera which was new on the market and the new gadget to have for instant photos. The mother was starting to get wary and suspicious of her husband as she would sometimes wake up with her underwear removed and have no recollection of removing it herself. She would ask him how did this happen and he would say that she must have been so tired and didn't remember removing them but it was becoming more regular. The mother did tell me that they had a super ser gas heater in their room and especially at night it would be lit and the bedroom heated up very quickly and her being exhausted would more or less instantly fall asleep. It was during these times that her underwear was being removed by the father and he was taking photographs of her naked in bed. She only discovered this when she found a Polaroid photo of herself in a trouser pocket of his. Things were starting to make sense to the mother then, During these years the mother had also had a few miscarriages which were all boys as she carried for long enough for them to be identified as boys. That was their marriage, Filled with suspicion, torment, rows, hard seasonal work and very few happy family memories and now he was taking indecent photographs of the mother. It wouldn't be until the next year that it was realised how affected and disturbed he was even though stripping his daughter and beating her for his and the mothers pleasure, frustration, heaped up anger or whatever excuse they had for it wasn't already disturbing enough.

In 1987 her mothers aunt was visiting from Boston and suggested that the family come to Boston for a few months and get some work while so that it would be like a working holiday. Her mother flew to Boston in March 1988 it was decided that the husband and 2 girls would follow a month later when she sent the fare back. A month later all four of them were reunited in these wonderment of a Boston city in America at the aunts house and the now 15 year old wasn't sure what they were doing there but it was just expected to get on with it and it was going to be an adventure. The mother had a job as a cleaner and the father found a job on a building site and both of them were making great money on this adventure while the older girl took care of her little sister during the day. 3 weeks into it the fathers father died back in Ireland and he returned on his own for the funeral and the children were left with her in Boston. The mother continued her job as a cleaner and would bring the smaller daughter with her to work because the older one now had a job now child minding with great pay also. This went on for another 2 months and then because the children's 3 month visas were coming to an end it was time for the children to return to Ireland, Their mother could stay because she had a 6 month visa. But there was an issue because both girls were on their fathers passport and so had no passports to travel and so after a lot of bureaucracy and needing official witnesses in Boston and Shannon airports to identify the girls they got home to Shannon airport with no adult accompanying them and taken by the guards at Shannon to be identified and handed over to their father. The beatings had stopped by now because she was older and there was no fight left in her and possibly because they were so busy being suspicious and fighting with each other that they were not bonded in their beating episodes of her anymore and in a way she felt safer when they were fighting with each other, Her soul had been drained from her and she just passed everyday as best she could.

Her one constant mission was that what happened to her would never happen to her sister. She spent her time making sure that the little one wouldn't cry, be loud, be annoying or any trouble to them because she was coming to 8 years of age and that's when she it started for the older girl. If she could help it, Nobody would ever do those things to the little one. It is hard to know how she would ever react if her little sister was ever dragged into that room for a beating but it certainly wouldn't have ended well for someone.

They had built a big house outside the town of Lisdoonvarna a number of years before this trip to America from the proceeds of a car crash that the mother and father were in and when they could they would buy supplies and furniture for it to become the family home and a new venture of a more manageable bed and breakfast if we ever left the hotel for a quieter life. It had never been lived in up to that because it was never finished or ready to move into. For the time that the girls had returned home to the father her mother would ring regularly to find out how they were doing and what was going on. The father had opened the bar in the hotel but again as money was coming in he was handing it out. The older was fully in charge of taking care of the younger sister and working in the bar also as their was no need for staff at such a quite time of the year. The father had started selling furniture, and anything he could just to have money and not work and she told her mother that things were being sold from the house and no ore was said about it. One morning at around 10am her mother walked into the hotel and immediately declared war on the father. She had been to the house out the road and seen that the majority of furniture, fixtures and fittings had been removed and sold. She didn't hold back and immediately called the guards to declare everything that was gone as stolen. When the mother returned to Ireland 6 weeks after the girls, the all out war started. He had sold everything that he could rather than get a job to pay bills. The bar of the hotel was open but whatever was coming in was also going out on loans to drinkers. She was happy that her mother was back but scared as this was a new heightened level of fighting. She had been responsible for her little sister at all times now, washing, cooking, cleaning, everything that was needed to take care of her. Now that her mother was back she followed her way because out of the two of her parents she felt somewhat safer and in control of her safety with her. The mother took the girls from the hotel and went to the unfinished and now unfurnished house with them to try and deal with the situation that faced her that day of her return, Everything of any value had been sold for pittance and she was devastated to return to such a mess. It got nasty, scary, intense and violent with both the parents and she honestly thought they would kill each other or the girls with the unrest and explosive tempers that they both had. Her mode had to be survivor and protector of herself and her sister. She was too young to leave and take her sister so she had to stay and choose the better of the two people to stay with, They stuck with the mother. Yes, she was the manipulative one but he was the more physical abuser and with an 8 year old sister to protect it was the better choice at the time.

Things got very agitated and vicious between them that year. She had come back to a house with nothing only the carcases of a kitchen, the oil fuel range and only a couple of the bathrooms fixtures and fittings left in the house. She had to raid the hotel on a couple of days when he wasn't there for necessities like blankets, sheets, pillows, towels, saucepans, cutlery, anything she and the girls could grab and carry to the house. One day when they were at the hotel the mother went into the attic to see if they were any family things that might be stored up ther. She was not prepared for what she found. The eldest girl was holding the ladder to the attic, the mother was in the attic with a torch and the little sister was sitting on a chair while the attic was being searched. While looking around the mother found a light switch and turned it on only to discover a tv, a video player, a high stool, 2 poloroid instant cameras, dozens of porn videos, dozens of porn magazines and a huge amount of indecent photos of the mother and her in a naked state while asleep. She started handing down all the stuff to the older girl to leave on the landing, it was crazy to her that all this stuff was up there. It now explained where he was disappearing to all those times he couldn't be found. Also there was another very disturbing discovery made. When the mother turned off the light she noticed that there was light coming into the attic from little holes on the floor of the attic which would be the ceiling of the bedrooms below it and she was trying to work out why there would be these holes in the floor of the attic. She lay down to see down and only when she seen where the holes were it dawned on her that the father was peeping into these bedrooms as each hole was strategically placed over these rooms to spy on people and what they were doing. That when they both realised how affected and sick he really was. That's when a whole new fear developed around what he would do now that his horrendous and sickening behaviour was discovered and now that his secret was out how would he react and deal with it. The mother left everything for him to find on the landing except for all the photos he had taken of her, she brought them with her and they went to the house in fear of how he would react. It didn't take long for the reaction, He arrived some time later threatening them that he would burn them out of it for being in the attic. There was a genuine fear that he would actually carry out his treat as he had gone ballistic and uncontrollable with temper and violence that evening. They had no car so a lot of walking back and forth to and from the house was taking place. He had a car and so would arrive at any time during the day and night for torment and rows with her which were physical and dangerous to be in. The ambulance was often called and the guards were often gone looking for him after he would break stuff in the house and or leave the mother or daughter with an array of injuries that sometimes required the mother to leave the girls there all night on their own while she was brought to the hospital 25 miles away to be treated for a fractured skull amongst numerous other injuries on numerous other occasions. The older girl would lock herself and her sister in the sitting room which had two doors out so that if need be she could scope up the small child and run out the front or back door to anywhere for safety. She would not sleep until the mother had returned after being treated and discharged herself from the hospital. There was a house phone but it was often pulled the out of the wall and the emergency services were getting very familiar with the family so there would be no way to send for help but to go to the neighbours house and call the guards. He had keys to the house and she had keys to the hotel. Everyday brought another row and more guards to the house, Everyday brought more trauma and disruption, Everyday brought uncertainty and upset because of the battle and fight that was going on everyday. The older daughter was starting to step in to the rows and get physically hurt by him as she was trying to protect her mother and this often led to her being left again on the floor with the brute force of a big strong man taking his anger out on her like she was to be silenced and kept down like she was before. More often there was whatever was to hand to beat her, a shovel, a brush, a handle, a bat, anything that could be hand held and add to the brutality of the beatings. She was often found in a heap somewhere in the house or outside in the garden badly beaten and in pain or sometimes in the field next door after trying to escape and save herself. One day it took the guards nearly 2 hours to find her unconscious in the long grass, and broken up and needing urgent help in case of internal injuries because she was barely alive. She had nothing but pure hate for this monster. Why can't this stop. Why can't he just leave them be. Why can't he stop stalking them. She was exhausted trying to cope and protect the frightened little sister everyday with the threat of social workers to take them away and separate them being thrown at them everyday. Again she just wanted peace and a secure place to be. The mother was drinking more trying to cope with what was going on, He was sneaking into to the house at all hours of the night and day checking to see where we were and what was going on. We would be woken at all hours of the night and walk into town to the hotel to stay in one of the rooms and we would be woken at all hours other nights to leave the hotel and go to the house. It was a cat and moose game with them. He was obsessed with what we were going and where we were, She was obsessed with hiding us because there was a genuine fear that he might wipe us all out in a fire or something similar. Something had to give, and it did.

As a result of all the times the guards would have to come to the house or the hotel after each episode of rows, fights, assaults and there would be many court cases to attend but because he would run to London every time and return unexpectedly he never showed for court to answer the many summons for assault or battery. The mother took out various barring and protective orders against him. There was a constant fear of being watched, a paranoia that he was watching from somewhere, a feeling that he was around somewhere, She could feel that someone was watching her or was she filled with such fear and tiredness that she mind was playing games with.

She got a job in a local hotel and the owner knew her and her family situation well so he had no hesitation giving her a job, the work was hard but she was well able for it and had no problem fitting into her role as a waitress or doing the hours. She would cycle from her house to the hotel at 6.30 every morning, return home around 11.30 and do whatever was necessary to try and make the house more liveable. There was painting and decorating, curtains to be hung, sort through whatever they managed to take from the hotel to make some sort of home in the house. Concrete floors, very little furniture but the bare necessities were there. That summer continued on and it was getting more tiring and harder for her to cope with working and trying to keep everyone safe and taken care of. She was earning £48 a week and a further £7 if she collected glasses in the nightclub on the Saturday nights. She would give her mother £40 of her wages every Monday for food, bills and whatever else was needed. There was no other money coming in at the time. Her escape every week was when a local rock band would play in a local pub and it was the place to be and meet all the other staff from the other hotels and have a great night out. Things were going well, He hadn't been around in 3 weeks and things like they were settling a bit. One day her boss called her up to the office for a chat and told her that her father was going to report him for allowing a 15 year old in to his other pub on Monday nights because she was underage. She wasn't drinking, She was only there to have some fun after a work filled week and now he was back and taking her few hours of fun and freedom from her. Is he trying to take everything from her, Is he trying to drive her completely mad. She continued to work but was not allowed to go to the pub anymore and that hurt because she saw very little of her friends then. It was work, Home and nothing else. He was still arriving out of the blue and trouble and upset was never far. As he had no car he would borrow his sisters car and use it to keep an eye on the house and our movements, She would sometimes meet him on the road parked up as she made her way home late at night after her work shift at the hotel. He was appearing in all sorts of places including parking up on another road and watching the house with binoculars. She was feeling the pressure build in her head for months and could feel herself not coping and becoming more and more overwhelmed and exhausted everyday.

She was resting one afternoon. She had worked all week and then done another shift collecting glasses at the nightclub on the Saturday night until 3 am before returning for the morning shift at 7 am, So right now a couple of hours sleep in the afternoon would sort her out before going back for the evening service, The sleep didn't last long.

When she awoke she could hear shouting and crashing going on downstairs. She knew straight away he was here. She got up and looked out the windows to make sure and her Aunts car was parked down on the road in front of the house, It was him. When was he ever going to leave them be, Why can't they just be left to get on with it, Enough was enough. She made her way downstairs and picked up a hammer that was beside the front door because she had been hanging pictures that her mother got in the charity shop around the house over the last few days and went outside. She walked down the path, down the steps, out the gate to the road and there she was at the Aunts car. She started to hit the windscreen, Several times hitting it but it wouldn't give, just smashed but stayed in place, she then smashed the lights in, the windows, the rear windows, the rear lights, anything that was glass was being hit and she was determined that he would never turn up in this car again. Somebody had to stop him, Somebody had to deal with it. She kept going, unaware of what was happening inside the house and completely unaware that he was racing towards her with a shovel.

Bang, she fell to her knees, still holding the hammer, She wasn't sure what had happened, all she knew in that moment that she had been hit hard on her back with an almighty force. Her mother was screaming to her to get into the house, her sister was screaming at him not to hurt her sister as she was trying to find her footing and get on her feet. Still reeling she got to her feet and received more and more whacks from the shovel, She managed to catch the shovel and throw it to one side. He was dragging around by her hair like a rag doll, hitting her, punching her, throwing her to the ground and kicking her wherever his foot landed. Her mother and sister were now on the road and trying to restrain him so as to give her a chance to escape. She moved as fast as she could, Barely able to catch her breathe. She thought just to hide herself somewhere that he wouldn't find her for him to finish killing her that day. She got onto the back low wall and into the hay field behind the house, She was trying to get to the wood to hide for a while. She looked back while trying to escape and there he was, following her faster than she was getting away. He caught up on her with a fury and violence in his eyes that she had seen before. She was exhausted and not able to fight back and had to take every punch, kick and slap that was put on her in that field where she wished to die, again.

She woke up in an ambulance, It had taken the guards a while to find her in the high grass because it was evening and it was getting dark rapidly. She had to be stretchered out of the field because she could barely walk or talk and was unconscious when found. She was taken care of in the emergency department and the following morning gathered what little strength she had, with stitched up wounds, and cuts and a face that was black and blue with one eye unable to open because of the swelling. A taxi brought her back to the house where the guards were in attendance again.

He had gone, Nowhere to be found, On the run back to London to wait it out until things settled. But unbeknown to her he did return at some stage to make a statement against her because a few weeks later she was summoned to be in court to answer charges of malicious to her aunts car. He had made a damning statement and she had to answer for it. Nothing had been made about her, no statement or complaint against him was lodged and the injuries she received because she was just content that he was gone, She was still 15 and very frightened to go to court.

The court was on locally in Lisdoonvarna so lots of local people were there for their own cases but also a lot more there to see this ridiculous case in court because never had a father taking his daughter to court and so it was hot gossip for the spectators. Her and her mother met with the solicitor outside and he informed them that he had been approached by her fathers solicitor to drop the case on one condition, and that condition was that the mother sign over her rights to the hotel there and then and the case would be dropped or risk the daughter being charged and being put in a juvenile home because of her crime with the car. Her solicitor was more than happy to take a chance in court as it was a first of its kind and he was not going to back down regardless of how the young one was feeling, which was terrified. Lots of cases were heard that morning and lots of guards and just a few solicitors that represented numerous clients that day and her case was the last of the day and the judge ordered everyone that had nothing to do with the case or the people involved to leave the courtroom, She was delighted as it took a fierce amount of pressure off her, Everyone that had to leave grudgingly did so. Her father was called to up to give his account of what happened while she listened and was disgusted that he described her as trouble, tormented, mentally affected and a nuisance to society and she needed to be locked up before she done something completely outrageous and unforgivable. She was doomed, He gave such a compelling performance about how he had to leave his home as his wife was an alcoholic, his daughter was a tearaway and his youngest daughter was in severe danger from her drunken mother and he couldn't stand by and do nothing, So his wife needed treatment for drink, his older daughter should be locked up and his youngest should go to his sister to be taken care of in Dublin. No more questions for him, He was told to sit down and she was called for. She slowly made her way up beside the judge, Doing her best not to cry with the sheer enormity and strain of what the judge must think of her and everyone else that was in that room. The judge sensed that she was scared and tried to put her at ease, and once she could control her breathing and not feel like she would collapse under the strain she started to tell the judge about what happened that day and why it happened, and told him that she was afraid most days, worried, doing her best at school and at work and that day she was exhausted and couldn't take any more upset and torment from her father and if he would just leave them alone to get on everything would be fine. The judge asked her gently and kindly about the other episodes that had taken place and she explained that someone will eventually get so badly hurt that there might be a death. He had finished asking her all he needed to know and asked that the Garda sergeant come forward and explain the situation and give his view. He said it was something he had never seen before in any family and yes someone will die if it doesn't stop and he also made a point of telling the judge all the injuries that she had received that day at the hands of her father with the shovel, She caught sight of him being very uncomfortable in his seat and his sister moving slightly away from him. Time for the judge to hand down his verdict. He said it was the saddest thing he had ever seen to see such a young girl brought in front for a time when she actually snapped and took the steps that she did out of desperation and despair, from exhaustion and worry while attending school and holding down a job, while doing her damn best by her mother and sister while he was out for revenge and destruction at any cost. She was very relieved to be bound to the peace for a year and the same sentence was handed to him but the barring order was updated for him to stay away from the family. He was filled with rage and swore that it wasn't the end. His sister wasn't too best pleased either when the judge told her to claim off the insurance instead of suing the young ones mother for the money to repair the damage she had caused to the car. No win that day for him, She was relived and happy to be able to go home from the court because she had expected to be taken away to some sort of imprisonment for her actions.

Things got back into a routine and she was happier as things were going well. But her mother was taking calls from him and that was pissing her off. She was always complaining to him that she needed some money for bills, for uniforms for the girls, for school fees, for food, for everything and anything. And he would send it through Western Union to be picked up at the Hostel in Doolin as they ran that service. He was employed running a pub in London so he was earning good money and could well afford to send something back. He started to book flights for the mother and the young sister to go to London and visit him. The older one was left to mind the house and take care of the dog and she was busy with work and school at that time. If she needed any groceries, like dog food, bread and milk, she could get them on credit in the local shop and the mother would pay for them on her return, she did get some other things like eggs or butter and she ran out of gas for the cooker one time and got a bottle on credit and delivered but her mother went ape shit at her for such an expense and she had to pay for that herself. These trips got more regular and longer and she was left more and more on her own at the house which was lonely but she did enjoy the peace that came with it. Her mother would ring every couple of days to check on things and that was all the contact there was. Sometimes she was brought over for a few days and she loved London with its big red buses, black cabs and an army of people everywhere. Very often on these trips there were rows with the parents and they would get bad and one night the mother hit him with a pool queue and she was arrested for assault and brought to the station for the night. The police in London don't tolerate any of that nonsense in their city. She was panicking because she didn't know if the mother would be released or not. The mother and daughters left London that day and swore never to go back for any visits. It wasn't long until he was sending money back again through Western Union and the mother and younger daughter were going regularly back and forth to London for longer trips each time. She was left on her own more and more to fend for her self and continue her last year in school. It was now Autumn and school was going alright, there was no work during the winter as the hotels closed after the season. She would stay the odd night at her friend Bernie's house in the next little village Kilfenora. It was nice to have the company and they would go to the local teenage disco and have great fun and even a slow dance and a shift with one of the boys from school. It was always fun and she was really her own boss now. The mother and younger sister were rarely home now and she started going out to the local pub more for games of pool and a drink if she could get served. There was no issue with getting served and so this became her weekends. An older man taht was a freiend of Bernie's would always give them a lift to Lahinch to the Claremont for the adult disco that was a great place to be and it was always a great night out. He started to leave Bernie home before leaving her home and some sort of a relationship was happening. They were sleeping together but it was a secret and not to be told to anyone. She kept that secret as she wasn't really comfortable with it anyway. It didn't last long anyway because she started finding excuses not to go out with that gang any more, She didn't want it to continue, She didn't want any more of it. Christmas was now here and her mother and sister were back for Christmas. Money was tight so Santa was to the little girl what was desired by her, usually a doll and accessories, she got 40 fags and the mother got a bottle of Brandy. She would go out to the local to meet friends for games of pool and a few drinks when she could. New year came in and a few days later on the 6th of January 1990 she was going out to celebrate her 17th birthday at the local pub. It was a Saturday evening, Her friends had invited her out to celebrate and she was going to have a good time. It was nothing major, just great friends meeting and cheering her birthday and making a fuss of her.

She didn't know it then but she was about to fall in love for the first time. She hadn't noticed that Billy had come into the pub that evening until he put a drink in front of her and kissed her on the cheek while wishing her a happy birthday. She blushed bright red, She thought she would pass out with the fluttering in her stomach, He told her to win the next game of pool because he was playing the winner and it better be her. Jesus, This man knew what he wanted and she liked it. She had noticed him before as he would come into the pub on the Saturday evenings after work and always made a point of saying Hello to her and asking how she was. She fancied him rotten, He had jet black hair, the biggest smile, a most gorgeous tan colour on him from working outside, and the body of a man, not like the wimpy boys in school, to her he was beautiful. He had a confidence about him, he was 27, 10 years older than her and that did not matter, He was exactly what she needed at that time. She liked that he was paying her attention and treating her nicely. He had a lovely way about him, He came across as gentle, kind and courteous. He would look at her in a way that she had never been looked at before. Here was this man that set her heart racing when she sees him and that melted her with his way of a gentle touch on her arm or saying goodnight to her before he would go and not see him until the following weekend. It kept her going knowing she would see him again the following weekend. No matter how bad things were at home she would be kept sane knowing that he would meet her and pay her the attention that she so craved and longed for. They started talking more from that night on and he invited her out for a drink and of course she said yes. There wasn't any where open only the local pubs for a drink so that is what they did and it was a whole new experience for her to be out in public with this man that was happy to be seen with her and that treated her so nicely. Ever courteous he would always drop her home, kiss her goodnight and see her the following weekend. A couple of weeks into the courting between them there was a reunion weekend coming up in Nenagh in Tipperary the following month and he was going and as it happened so was she and her mother and a whole gang of people from Lisdoonvarna. She would be staying overnight in a B and B, it was all very grown up. She was bursting with excitement for the night away at the event in the hotel, It was going to be fabulous. She went to Tipperary early that day, the younger sister was gone to her cousins house to stay so nothing to worry about, Just go and enjoy herself. She checked into her single room at the B and B, just up from the hotel, and spent time getting ready, until it was time to go to the hotel for the dinner dance. Her and her friends arrived at the hotel and there Billy was, waiting for her, he took her hand and greeted her with a kiss, again she thought she would melt. They sat together that night and had a very relaxed, enjoyable, happy night together. They were on the dance floor, slow dancing and she completely fell for him, hook' line and sinker, that night. He held her, he caressed her, he whispered to her, She thought she would die a happy girl if she didn't wake up tomorrow. He walked her back to the B and B and without anything being persuaded upon her they were in her room, kissing, holding and wanting each other there and then. It would be their first time together and there was no pressure, it was loving, slow, sensual, wonderful and she never wanted it to end. He stayed the night with her and she didn't care if her mother found him there with her. He held her all night and she slept with an ease and contentment like never before. Saying goodbye to him the following morning was fine because she knew they were together now and she was top of the world. Nothing else mattered to her in that night and day. Back to the normality of home, the last few months in school, back to work in the hotel but having a proper relationship with Billy was her focus and her saving grace. She was busy but they would meet at weekends and spend time together with friends on nights out and alone time when they could. Those were the times she craved as she had fallen hard for him and was in love with him and she knows he felt the same. She was happy with her life right now, She was with someone that she adored, she was nearly finished school, she was busy working and getting to keep her wages as her mother and sister were in London most of the time and she had some great friends at her job. Everything was going well for her except, she had a recurring fear, she hadn't had a period in a while and deep down she just knew she was pregnant but could not admit it to herself. She continued as best she could, Hiding it as much as possible but she had to tell Billy. It was becoming obvious and he was noticing but she would pass it off as weight gain but it came to a stage where it couldn't be passed off any more. She told Billy that she was pregnant and to which he responded that, that's ok, and we could take care of it together and it will be fine. Billy as always was calm, cool and no panic about it. She was in such dread and despair before that but now it was going to be ok with Billy by her side. Her mother had been in London for about a month now and had summoned her to go to London to join them for a few days. With complete fear she arrived in London and with one look they both knew she was pregnant straight away, and again all hell broke loose.

The shouting and questions and roaring at her was relentless. She was trapped and there was no escape. They were disgusted with her and had no issue telling her so. All she wanted was to get back on a plane and get home to Billy. When they had settled down and realised it was too late for an abortion for her, which she would never have consented to anyway, they had to come up with a plan. The most bizarre and disturbing thing that was mentioned was that her father announced that she return home immediately in case anyone thought it was his. Is he completely twisted to think that anyone would think it was his. To this day she cannot figure that thought process out. A few days later, the mother and 2 daughters returned to Lisdoonvarna and it had been decided that she would not make contact with anyone. If she did drive to the shop she was to remain in the car while her mother or sister went in and if anyone approached her while she was in the car she was ordered to make her excuses and drive away. She was to stay indoors at all times, and never to be seen by any local person until this was over. Hide it at all costs. A local social worker was summoned and he made arrangements for ClareCare to be contacted, They were a group of social workers in Ennis that would know what to do about this pregnancy and how to deal with it and how to organise the adoption of her bastard. That was the language that was being used around her, Whore and bastard repeated to her constantly. A lady that was a lay nun of sorts called to visit her at her now prison, She was kind and gentle and took things slowly with her. She organised for a private Doctor to see her in Ennis and she went to her first medical appointment in early July, It was thought that she was and it was determined that she was 7 months pregnant, that meant it wasn't Billy's. There was no hope now, for her, for her and Billy, for nothing good to come of this only heartache and misery for all concerned. She told Billy about the baby not being his and yet he wanted to stay with her, She had to let him go, It was an impossible situation for them both, She loved him so she had to leave him and not entangle him in the mess she was in. It broke her heart into a million pieces to have to leave him but it was for the best. She was attending monthly doctors appointments in Ennis and then they progressed to fortnightly appointments. While all this was going on she was working doing Bed and Breakfast at the house with her mother. It was a basic B and B and of clean standard and it was going well. They were doing the best they could, And it was hard work but she did enjoy meeting people in the house. The lay nun would call to the house to see how she was and for discussions about the next stage of the adoption. The new plan was that for the last month of the pregnancy she would go to Galway and stay with a family, and help them with the household and children until she went into labour, had her baby and returned home to Clare. She was uneasy with the idea but went with it for peace sake, the mother was getting more and more paranoid about people finding out about her and the pregnancy and there were a couple of extra meetings with the nun to talk about prospective adoptive parents. She didn't think that she would be as involved as she was with the choosing of the parents but it was of huge benefit for her to be involved in the choice. One couple stood out to her, The new Mum had her own playschool and her husband was a school bus driver. They had no other children and so her baby would be their first if she picked them. She liked the sound of them because the new mum worked with babies and small children and her baby would be with the new mammy all the time and the dad would be home at good times to help with the baby so the decision was them. She was asked if she would like to meet them and refused because there was a fear in her that if she ever saw them somewhere she would not cope. It was now September in Lisdoonvarna and the start of the Matchmaking month in Lisdoonvarna. She was tired, lonely and depressed with the thoughts of meeting her baby only for the baby to be taken away and going to someone else. The plans changed for her to go to Galway as she was needed at the Bed and Breakfast in Lisdoonvarna so she was happy to stay in her familiar surroundings. The festival ended as quick as it came around, and all was quite in the first week of October 1990. She was booked into Limerick hospital to be induced as they felt it was the right time. The nun brought her to the hospital and checked her in and she was left in the care of the nurses and doctors to get on with it. Nothing was going to happen until tomorrow, and she spent most of her time in her bed afraid and upset in the situation that she was in. Her mother was ringing the nurses station every hour looking for updates and was always informed that there would be no news tonight but to ring back tomorrow evening when they would be expecting things to be moving. The following morning she was told that they would be inducing her early for an afternoon delivery and she was rigged up to monitors, she was given a pessary to start labour. After a few hours there was contractions but not strong enough for her to be brought to the labour ward. After a long day that felt like forever it was night time and she could rest in between the contractions that were getting stronger, or maybe just stronger to her because she was physically worn out. The next morning arrived all to soon and a doctor appeared to tell her that he was going to break her waters and that the baby would be here today. Her mother was still ringing the hospital late into the night previous demanding that they get this child out of her and get her home, She was embarrassed and tormented by her actions. Today was the day and she was not prepared emotionally for the day ahead. Her waters were broken and things took a big turn, she was soon in full labour with only a gas to help her with the horrendous pain that was hitting her harder and more regular as the day went on. They informed her numerous times that her mother was ringing again but this time she was on the way to the hospital. This gave a sense of panic, She didn't want her there, She didn't want anyone there, She just wanted the baby to be born and to make sure that they were ok, On her own, By herself. That didn't happen, The mother had arrived around midday and somehat worse for wear with some drink in her. She demanded to be in the delivery room, She kept roaring at her with each contraction to get that child out, to push it out, to come on and get it over with. She was doing her very best, She was struggling because she was so tired and upset with this loud lunatic of a mother shouting and trying to take over while she was doing her level best to cope giving birth. The baby finally made an appearance at 1.30 pm in the afternoon, a beautiful baby boy she was told, she didn't get a glimpse of him as the mother was shouting to get the child out of the room immediately as he was for adoption and she was not to even touch him. The nurse just left with him, She was told that the nun was outside and that she would accompany him down to the nursery. She was in hell, Just given birth and didn't see him, or touch him and a mother telling her to hurry up and get well and get herself back home as quick as possible. Get out of there as quick as you can and leave it all behind you. The mother was leaving to get the bus back home for 5.30 pm. She was put into the cruellest ward possible, A 6 bedded ward for new mothers and their babies. 5 mothers were there with their babies and husbands/partners and she was just there alone. She was torn apart mentally, upset, emotional and couldn't stop crying, sometimes crying so hard she couldn't breathe and had a pain in her chest like her heart had been ripped out. The nun landed in to see her late that night, and told her how beautiful he was, how healthy he was and would she like to see him. Of course she wanted to see him, she was aching to see him, to hold him, to smell him, to breathe him in. The nun brought her to the nursery and she was introduced to her son. He was truly beautiful, He was so small, He was amazing, What a wonderful feeling to have him in her arms. She spent a whole hour just drinking him in and admiring every little bit of him, and then it was time to leave, The nun had obviously got some sort of special permission as a nurse came in to take him and feed him and put him to bed. She was grateful that she had that precious peaceful hour with him. The nun told her that he was being baptised the next morning in the hospital chapel and she was to name him and attend the baptism if she wished. Off she went to bed with joy in my heart that she would get to see him in the morning again. Morning came all too quickly, she was tired and sore but excited to go to the chapel for the christening but dreading the time going forward as she knew she had to leave the hospital later that day and when would she see baby Patrick Joseph again, if ever. The nun arrived full of the joys as usual but sensitive to her, and they went to the chapel and waited there. Baby Patrick Joseph was wheeled in inside a little cot unit. He was just truly beautiful and very content. Is was over in a few minutes with just the bare blessing but it was nice to have him christened and know that he was feeding well and doing good. It was getting to mid morning and it was time for the nun to take the baby to his foster home somewhere. Everything was ready for him there and he was expected to arrive that day. She was doing ok until it was time to say goodbye to him. She went down to the nursery with the nun and he was all dressed in a blue baby grow, just fed, winded and a dry nappy on. He was in his element, Oblivions to what was going on around him. She was holding on as best she could, She was dying inside, the most beautiful part of her ever was right in front of her and she had to let him go. If there was any hint of another option available to her she would have kept him. If he could be kept with love alone he would be staying with her. She returned to her room and was all packed and ready to go herself. She ordered a taxi from the ward and left in a haze of tears, confusion and exhaustion, the taxi brought her home to Lisdoonvarna where she went in and down to her room and just lay on her bed only 24 hours after giving birth and in a lot of pain because of the stitches she had received after having her baby. Her mother knew she was home and yet nobody checked on her. She had a very bad night of no sleep with the wondering of where her baby was and the nightmares when she would fall asleep. Morning came around all too soon and she got up and made her way to the kitchen for a strong cup of tea. Her mother was in fowl humour and was telling her to just move on now and get over it, And to get some proper clothes on and go to the shop for a few things. The idea behind the trip to the shop was so that she would be seen by the locals and so any rumours about her could be dispelled by her being out in public. Being out was the last thing she wanted but she went. Grabbed a tracksuit bottoms and a baggy sweatshirt for the trip and so it was done.

The following day the Queen of the Burren festival was starting in Lisdoonvarna at the end of the tourist season. There was music and social dancing in most of the pubs at certain times over this last weekend. One of the highlights was that everyone would go to Fanore to O'Donohues pub on the Sunday afternoon for a few hours. Her mother demanded that she put on the tightest jeans she could find so as to hide any tummy that might be there and to kill all rumours of a pregnancy and do herself up and get ready to go there for the afternoon. She did not want to go near it as she was still recovering, very emotional and just now coping at all. But it was easier to do as she was told against her will than to be told how still useless she was and to get over it. Off they went to Fanore which is one of the most beautiful drives in the whole world to the music and dancing that was on. She gathered herself up and walked in behind her mother who was glammed to the nines and had something to prove to everyone there. As she walked in and headed for the bar her heart leaped out of her chest because Billy was there, and he never took his eyes off her as she got to the counter. She ordered the drinks for her mother and herself and she could feel a lot of eyes on her. She was very uncomfortable but she was doing her best to blend in. She caught Billy's eyes as she looked around, She panicked, She wanted to leave right there and then, too late he was headed straight for her. He casually walked up to her and asked her for a dance, It was a waltz so he took her by the hand and led her onto the dance floor and pulled her close to him. All eyes in that room were on them and she was anxious and not sure what to do but just go with it. He pulled her closer and gently holding her asked if she was ok. He knew that she had the baby, He just didn't know the details or when. Once he asked it, She could feel herself welling up to cry, she could feel his arms of comfort around her, she was aching for her baby, she was heartbroken and so upset in that moment that she thought she would pass out. Billy took her hand again and led her outside where she just let go and cried her heart out. There was no judgement from him, just holding her while she let go with her tears. He told her he was taking her home because it was rest she needed. There wasn't much said on the way home, he held her hand while he drove with the other. They got to the house and he turned to her and reassured her that everything will be ok, to get some rest and he would see her the following weekend and they would spend some time together. He kissed her and said goodbye and it somehow healed her a little because for the first time in a long time it felt like it was going to be ok. That nice feeling didn't last long. The mother arrived back sometime later giving out about how she was left in the pub on her own and how dare she leave her there. She didn't care, she had something to look forward to in seeing Billy again, Little did she know but her father was on his way back from London that week.

Her father arrived as if to make sure that she had the baby and that he was gone to foster care. He was an absolute asshole about it all. He had a look to her that was of disgust and humiliation towards her and her bastard secret. The nun was calling to the house that week to do a follow up on her and the mother and father were such different people in the nun's presence that they were unrecognisable to her. The meeting was going well with stories of how well Baby Patrick was doing and that his adoptive Mum and Dad had met him and how excited and thrilled they were with him. It was going so well until the nun mentioned that a visit was possible to see him in his foster home. Dear Jesus a visit would be incredible to her, but she found herself searching the faces of her mother and father for their reaction and praying silently that it would happen. It was agreed that the visit could go ahead and the excitement was overwhelming. It was to happen next week and she was literally counting down the hours for it to take place. She had mentioned that she was meeting Billy the next weekend and of course it was met with an array of bad opinion that she was going out to get pregnant again, as if, she needed someone that she knew just to care for her with no judgement and no agenda. She did go out and meet Billy and they had a drink in the local, went to the chipper and parked up on the main street and just talked, for what seemed like hours. They had missed each other as they hadn't seen each other in 3 months, but they somehow just fell back in with each other so easily. She went home that night feeling a whole more grounded and settled and excited for the week ahead, She was starting to feel some sort of normal again.

It was the day of the meeting at the foster parents house. She had bought a card and written some things to Baby Patrick about how sorry she was and how much she loved him and would always love him. And also had bought him a little teddy to give him when she got to see him. Her father drove them to the foster parents house which was an hour away and the nun was there as well. Her presence was helping her to relax a little bit, she was a ball of nerves, so anxious, and afraid that the foster parents would look at her in a disgusted way for giving up her baby, She was worried about being judged again there, but the excitement was taking over her more so than the worry. They arrived and were welcomed into a real family home. It had a comforting air about it. The lady led them into the sitting room where the ladies husband was and the nun, and there in a bassinet was a little bundle sleeping gently. They said their hello's but she never took her eyes off the bundle. Tea was offered and made and the bundle must have been disturbed by the noise of them in the room and started to mooch about and wake up. His foster mother picked him up and unwrapped him from his blanket, and there he was, He had grown, he was stretching and taking his time to familiarise himself with what was going on. She was asked if she would like to hold him, of course she would, she was actually dying to hold him and see him and just take him in. His foster mother was gone to get a bottle for him as he was due a feed. The bottle arrived and it was assumed by her holding the baby that she should hand him over to the foster mother for the bottle but instead she handed the bottle over and told her to go ahead and give it to him. This did not bode well with either her mother or father but the nun could see the tension and was willingly keeping them in conversation in order to distract them and give her the time and space to enjoy this wonderful interaction with her baby. It felt so natural to her, it was beautiful and so wonderful to see him. He had grown, he had changed a little, and he was gorgeous and so quite and content, He was truly beautiful. The mother and father and her little sister all got to hold him and they both put on a show of how lovely he was and how it was for the best that this be the last time to see him. Even in this wonderful home they managed to ruin it with their thoughts and opinions of what happens and when. It was time to go as the atmosphere was changing, it must have been because they saw the love and hurt in her eyes as she held him and they realised she didn't want to let go and in case she said it out loud they had to get her out of there. Not a word was spoken to her on the return journey home only a discussion of how long would it be before he was officially gone to be adopted and how much better off everyone will be when that happens. Better off for who, She was in turmoil in the back of that car, she wanted so much just to be able to return to that wonderful home and be able to take him to a home of their own and the two of them disappear away from all the evil and discontent and disgust that surrounded them both by her hateful parents in the front of that car.

Things pretty much continued as normal as they could. Her mother and sister were going back and forth to London to the father while she stayed at home but some trips she took to London too when she was asked. Her and Billy continued and were going great, they were in a proper relationship and she was content and happy with that aspect of her life. He treated her well and she truly loved him. On her return from one of the trips there was a letter waiting for her asking her to make contact as soon as possible with the nun in ClareCare as she had some news for her. A little panic set in as what could it be. She rang the following day and the nun asked if they could meet somewhere as she had to tell her something. There was a fear in her after that contact because she felt that something was wrong, It was. They met and the nun informed her that little Patrick was great but there was a problem, One of his ears were not developing and there was a possibility that he could be deaf and if he was deaf then he would have to stay in foster care and possibly end up in care for always because nobody would want a deaf child. This unsettled her greatly, she couldn't let him go to care for the foreseeable future, she had to take him herself, it was meant to be. He had to go for tests and she would be kept informed of the results and how he was doing. It was a very fast process as the results were in 3 days later, He was perfectly fine, she was so relived and thankful that he was ok. She now had huge conflicting thoughts of keeping him or letting him go. Keeping him was becoming more and more of a bad decision for him and her as she felt she couldn't completely protect him from the vicious minds of her parents. They would somehow poison him and turn him into a victim of their evil and she had to protect him from living a life like that. She had to remind herself that no matter how much it hurt to admit it there was two people just dying to adopt him as their own and nourish and protect him as much as she did and those two people were in limbo right now wondering if he was to be their's. The nun was pushing for a decision, her parents were tormenting her everyday towards the better decision for them but ultimately the decision to be made had to be in Baby Patricks best interest and where he would be protected and loved. She lost a piece of her heart the day she signed the final papers for his adoption but it was the best and safest place for Baby Patrick to be.

Again she was back working everyday at the house, decorating, gardening, painting, cleaning, in general getting the house into shape as her mother had decided that she was going to do Bed and Breakfast and everything had to be got ready for the season of 1991. her father was back and forth to London and plenty of rows still with her parents fighting all the time and still guards in and out of their lives. It was turbulent and a constant wonder as to what might happen in each day. Her and Billy were only seeing each other once a week into the tourist season as they were both so busy working but they had great nights out when they could. Things got back into a more even keel when October came in and it was all going great, There might even be a future in it. Coming up to the Christmas season a good friend of her's had started asking her about her relationship with Billy and what he was like and of course she was full of praise for him and how wonderful he was and how great they were getting on, She didn't realise that her friend was simply gathering information on Billy so that she could move in and have him. She wasn't aware of anything until one day her friend told her that she had been out with Billy and that they had a great time and that she would be seeing him from now on. They hadn't actually been out but it was enough for her to know that she was going after him and she would get him. But why, What the fuck was she talking about, She couldn't be going anywhere with him because he was her's and they were going out that weekend, But she knew it was over because that one could get any man she wanted to, This one came from an affluent family and had her own business, her own car and none of the torment, need or love for Billy that came from the messed up one he was with. It didn't last long with them two anyway. That one wanted him, she got him and she threw him to the kerb when she was finished. There was no going back for Billy and her, once the friend had taken him, and he went, it could never be the same, She had now lost Billy, her first true love, and a one time friend.

She decided that she needed a good break from everything after Christmas. She needed a change of location and atmosphere. She was heartbroken and needed something new to focus on. She decided she would go to London as there was a job going in her fathers pub. She had no better options at that time so she took it and went. She was staying over the pub as the job came with accommodation, It suited her perfect, She wasn't answerable to anyone only herself. Her mother wouldn't be coming over because she now was staying at home to mind the house and have the younger sister in school more often. Things were good in London, She settled in nicely, worked hard and went off touring London on her days off. There was little or no interaction between her and her father, she just got on with things and as big as London is it can be a lonely place to be. She enjoyed her independence and time there but she had a hankering to go home, it wasn't long until that happened. Her aunt that lived in London died later that year and she went home for the funeral which was at the start of the tourist season in Lisdoonvarna. She met up with friends and she decided to stay home for now and see what happens. It was busy in the B and B and she was kept going working away. She would see Billy the odd time and have a drink with him but they was no romance any more with them, just good pals now. She didn't have the time or patience for just any man any more but she was still looking for love and along it came in the guise of Jarlath, a musican with a band in Lisdoonvarna whom she had known since she was a child as he was 13 years older than her. She was now 19 and he was 32, the older, more steady, quite man suited her. It was a comfortable, steady thing they had going and it was reliable and consistent with them both, there was no lighting bolts but it was nice and easy and went on for a year and a half but it wasn't going anywhere and so it finished quite amicably. Not much was going on in her life now. It was just living week to week, meeting friends, going out, working hard and home was still shit with her mother drinking and turning on her regularly and getting worse each time. It soon was her 21st birthday and she didn't celebrate it as she had never had a birthday cake or a birthday party so why would her 21st be any different. But she did go out that day with her 2 friends David and Mark and they went to Doolin pier and sat on the rocks with a flaggan of cider and toasted her birthday, It was a nice way to mark the day. She got home later that day and went to her room which was on the 3rd floor and just lay on her bed to sleep. Her mother arrived into the room drunk and shouting and roaring that how dare she fuck off that day birthday or no birthday. Her mother dragged her from the bed and pushed and dragged her onto the hall and then pushed her and she fell down the stairs. She lay there for a minute as her mother roared at her from the top of the stairs that she was only a cunt and just fuck off and die, The mother was now at the bottom of the stairs kicking her and screaming at her how worthless she was. Maybe she actually was worthless and stupid, and a waste of space and just not meant for this world. The only thing available to her later that night was paracetamol for the pain she had all over after the fall down the stairs. It was a large tub of them and she didn't stop at 2, she swallowed about 20 and lay in her bed and prayed to just leave this world because she could not take any more and couldn't keep being such a disappointment to her mother and family of course. She woke up not too long later vomiting and with terrible stomach pain. Fuck it, she was still here and her stomach was rejecting the tablets, Was there nothing she could do right. She was really sick all the next day and her mother let her be in case it was a vomiting bug she had and might pass it on, That suited her fine, Just to be left alone and cry to herself. She was down in the dumps alot of the time but always put on a smile as that was the way to do things, Just accept your life as it is and get on with it, and that is how she lived, Not expecting anything from anybody, Doing the best she could to survive and stay there to care for her sister, Hoping that Baby Patrick was doing ok, She was lucky because she got updates from Patricks Mum and Dad on a yearly basis, She still ached for her baby boy. Not too long after her suicide attempt she was on a night out in Ennistymon and a little drunk. She met Paul that night, Paul was to her a gorgeous man, full of charm and such a flirt, again he was someone she had known most of her life and he was 13 years older than her. But it was the start of something good as far as she was concerned , She is still not sure if it was the best time to meet him or the worst time to meet him because only 2 weeks earlier had tried to leave this world. She fell hard for him over a number of weeks, She couldn't help herself, He told her all the right things and made all the right moves, gave her a look that wanted her, got her when she was at her most vulnerable and off guard. 3 weeks into it she was packing a bag and moving in with Paul at his brothers house in Lahinch to a lot of objection from her mother but she needed to get out before she was carried out in a coffin. Everything was great, She was out, free, and with a man she again loved and wanted to stay with forever. The time of year that it was everyone was out of work as it was out of tourist season and there was no work available at the time so once a week people collected their dole money from the unemployment exchange in Ennistymon and a lot of them would go drinking on that day. Paul and his brother were drinkers and would always go drinking for a few days at a time but she would always buy groceries and fuel for the house for the 3 of them as that was important for her and she was living there rent free. Paul would make Bodhrans, a musical drum propular in traditional irish music, so he would have a little extra drinking money. The drinking wasn't too bad in her eyes, she loved him and that's all that mattered. He would do some work for people when required but it was never of any benefit to him. He was home when he was broke, and she loved those times because they were together, and enjoying the time together but he was always looking forward to his next session. Paul wasn't very popular in the pubs as he was always getting loans, and caging free drinks from people, always on the lookout for himself and drink. A year into it he started not coming home on the days he would collect his money and she wouldn't see him for 2 or 3 days at a time. His brother always covered for him saying that he had gone to Ennis to meet up with old friends and they probably ended up going on a session. It soon transpired he was with staying with an ex girlfriend. This broke her heart everytime he didn't come home but he always reassured her that he slept on her couch and she was only a drinking buddy and she fell for his excuses everytime and always took his explanation and apology until it happened again. She loved him and forgave him everything, no matter what he did and he knew it and knew exactly how to treat her and convince her that he did love her and want her. She had no contact with home and that suited her, She couldn't go back to that house and try and function, she done the best she could and carried on as well as she could. For her at the time she was in love and that's all that mattered to her. Her mother met her in the town one day and was as nice as could be to her which was completely unsettling to her. She was pleasent and they went to the pub for a drink and it was ok and calm. She didn't want anymore meetings like that as she felt her mother was closing in on her. It wasn't too long until her mother starting calling to the house where she was living with Paul and this was horrible for her as the mother always had an agenda and a plan that was only beneficial for her own uses. The mother made a great effort with Paul, She would make it her business to be in town on dole day and meet him somewhere along the line. She would promise him work and a place to live if he would convince the daughter to move back home but with everything in her she refused to go back to the hell hole. Paul was trying hard with her when he could to convince her that it would work, she was never convinced that it was ever going to work, Why couldn't her mother just leave them be. A year and a half later with Paul she wasn't feeling great and she had a feeling that she might be pregnant. She went to the doctors without saying anything to Paul and she had to take a blood test to find out and wait a few days for the results. Of course Paul was missing for the few days while she was waiting on him to return and for news of her blood test. She went to the doctors and sure enough it was positive with an estimated due date the following May. She was excited, but upset because she wanted him home to tell him the news, It was brilliant news but she was anxious as to how Paul would receive the news. She didn't have to wait long to find out as Paul returned the next day, all apologies and she ever forgiving as usual. She told him the news and he was delighted that there was a baby on the way. He told her everything that she wanted to her and how wonderful life was going to be for the three of them from now on. She was happy that he took the news so well and excited that she was now going to have her own little family to take care of, to love and protect. Of course the mother found out soon after and was becoming more involved by visiting more and mentioning that they both should move up to her house and take the mobile at the back of the house as their own space to live. They both could work for the mother getting the house ready for the season ahead and it would all be great as far as the mother was concerned. She was not to quick to go with the idea, but when Paul ws back to disappearing for a few days at a time and leaving her alone and pregnant it started to be the only option available to her in her situation and she somehow thought that it would settle Paul into the family life that she wanted for the three of them. They moved up to Lisdoonvarna in early 1996 and it was ok at first. Paul was painting and doing odd jobs and maintenance about the house and she was kept busy getting rooms ready for the season ahead. He started going away for 2 nights each week to Ennistymon and staying at his brothers house and returning all apologies again to her when he was broke and each and every time she always took him back. He started drinking at the house a lot more as the mother daily drinking so it was perfectly natural to him to have a drink as well. He would always do whatever had to be done and get paid that evening from the mother so he could buy a bottle of gin and a packet of cigarettes. The two of them would sit up and get drunk together,

She was just happy to have him there most of the time now as she was coming up on her due date soon. It was up to her to have everything in place for the baby as Paul took care of himself and when he would ask her for money and she told him it went on taking care of them with groceries and things for the baby that was arriving soon he would shout and give out about how much she was spending even though she hadn't much money and was doing the best she could to take care of them and have things in place for the baba. She felt he would be happier and not drink as much when the baby came. Her due date came and went and the hospital decided she would have to go in for the baby to be induced. She was given a date and she was ready for this baby to arrive as she was so fed up towards the end and in a lot of discomfort. The day before she was going to the hospital to be induced Paul went to get his money and did not come back that night, She was so upset because he promised her he would with her went she went to the hospital but instead a family friend dropped her off at the door at admissions and she checked herself in to have the baby. She was so sad, and afraid as she was there on her own and trying to cope as best she could with the lovely nurses that were taking care of her but it was frightening for her. The plan was that she would be induced the following morning and hopefully her baby would be here by the following afternoon. She had an uneasy night, one of excitement to finally meet her baby and one of fear in case anything went wrong. Her mother was now ringing regularly to the nurses station and no matter how many times they told her that there would be no baby until the afternoon she still rang every half hour, she was probably well drunk already early into the day, all she could do was apologise for her mother ringing so frequently. By 1 o clock that afternoon she was well on her way to having the baby, in labour but on her own, she was scared and for some reason she was afraid that she wouldn't get to see her baby. Her waters hadn't broke so they were broke for her and things certainly kicked off from there. The midwife that was looking after her was a lovely lady but was becoming more and more frustrated with the amount of phone calls that were coming in about her patient, all she could do was apologise for her mothers behaviour and hopefully the baby would come soon so the calls might stop. No phone call from Paul though. Here she was on her own in a room with strangers and about to have her baby with no support or help from anyone in her life, She never felt more alone. A bouncing baby boy arrived not long later and he was perfect, He had all his toes, his fingers, all was perfect with him but the overwhelming emotion hit her hard and she couldn't stop crying. Eventually she was on the ward and the nurses wanted to take the baby to the nursery so that she could rest for a while but she wouldn't let them take him, some fear was in her that she wouldn't see him again. She slept a while and when she woke up the nurses had taken her baby to the nursery so she could rest. She went and got him and brought him up to her bed in the ward and just spent time checking on him, checking he had all his fingers and toes, He was beautiful and just a perfect baby. She was really enjoying this alone time with him and she spent hours just drinking him in and admiring him. She slept a lot easier that night, he was in his little trolley cot by her bed and she was ready with a bottle, nappies and winding when he awoke during the night for his feeds. Paul and her mother had rang after the birth, they were told it was a boy but she had asked the nurse to say she was resting as she just wanted to be left alone with her boy and enjoy him and not lose any time talking to anyone on the phone. She got up the following day with a pride and happiness about her and was in full new mother mode, She was loving her new role. Nobody else mattered to her right now. She had to stay in the hospital that day and would be going home the next day. She was happy to stay in the hospital another day as she had more alone time with her little man. The next day came all too soon and she was all packed and ready to go when a friend collected her to bring her home to Paul, who had eventually returned to the house when she was giving birth at the hospital, and her mother and sister. She arrived home and introduced Paul to his son, she was so upset and annoyed that he hadn't been with her when she had the baby but he started crying when he held his boy and again she forgave him everything. This was a new start for her and her little family now and everything was going to be great from here on in. It all went great for the first 2 weeks, Paul was there to help her with the baby, who was now called Steven, after being a Shane for around 3 days but it didn't suit him, She was back working for her mother as the season had started and people were were around the area so tourist a plenty about the place. They got into a routine that worked, but she was exhausted with feeds during the night and then ready for 7 every morning with a forced smile on to do the b and b while Paul kept an eye on the baby in the mobile home. When breakfast was over she would get the baby and feed him, dress him for the day and spend some time with him until everyone had checked out and she could start turning over the rooms for the next guests. She was trying to juggle everything and she needed the money for all the necessities that came with having a new baby. Paul was drinking but not as bad as he normally would, He was in love with the little man Steven, he told her everyday how much he loved her and was doing well so it was the best it could be for the time being. About 2 weeks into this new normal Paul went to collect his dole and after promising her faithfully that he would be back he failed to come home that night. She knew in her heart of hearts that he was on a bender and she wouldn't see him for a few days, she was angry, upset and fed up, especially as everything was going so well. A couple of days later she took Steven for a drive to Doolin to have a walk by the sea and go for a coffee to O' Connors pub. The fresh air at the sea done them both the world of good and it felt great just to hear the sea and taste the salt in the air, Her favorite place in the world is to sit on the rocks there and just breath in the beauty of the Cliffs of Moher in the distance and to look towards the Inisherr

Island and think of getting over there for a long overdue day trip. Enough dreaming, she drove to O' Connors and carrying Steven in his carry seat, and his baby bag, she was in the pub eyeing a seat by the fire and ordering her coffee. She was a little bit overwhelmed as it was her first time out with Steven and she was fumbling. She heard a familiar, kind voice, Can i take the baby and get a seat for us, he said, It was Billy, Where the hell did he come from. She hadn't seen Billy in 3 years and here he was carrying her new baby to a seat where they could sit and have a drink and a catch up. She was blind sided for a moment, but she got settled with her coffee and Billy with a pint and sat there and told each other of all that was going on in each others lives. Billy was home in Doolin for a few days with his girlfriend. Billy was going to be a Daddy in a few months as his girlfriend was pregnant and it was all going great for him. She was delighted for him, he deserved to be happy and he would be an amazing dad. He was so excited talking of his new baby and all that was ahead for him. He wanted to know if she was ok and were things going well for her, she lied of course and told him all was very well. They spent a good hour just chatting, catching up and she was enjoying just being out and the company she was in. Ever the gentleman Billy helped her to the car with the baby and whatever else she had, They said goodbye and it had been great for her that they were able to be so easy with other with their history together. She returned home and that was that. Paul returned a few days later and in the same repetitive move, He apologised, She forgave him and that's the way it was and she didn't know it then but this was her life now, Her baby Steven and Paul were her priority but she was nobody's first care. She always believed that Paul loved her when he said it because she certainly loved and adored him so he must mean it. She had to know that he loved her, she had to believe it because she needed to be loved and to be needed. The one boy she knew who did love her was her little boy Steven, No matter how bad her day was she had him, he had a smile that melted her heart and loved cuddles with her baba everyday. All was ok, Things were the same everyday, Summer season busy and winter season was quite with trips to Kildare to see her grandparents, Peter and Maisie. She loved going to Kildare because her Grandad Peter was a gentleman and she adored him in everyway. He had a softness and kindness about him and she and him always got on great with a great love between him, She still misses him to this day. If he saw or heard her mother giving out to her or being bad to her he would step in and put his daughter her place and remind her to leave his grandaughter alone. He was getting older now and not as able as he once was so the visits to Kildare more frequent. She was the driver and it was a drive of 4 hours to Kildare but it was worth it to see her grandparents everytime. Paul would go on those trips to Kildare when he was home with her and not off for days at a time. She liked these trips as they were a break from the normality of home. They would go for a drink at the local pub and she already knew a lot of the locals from her years of visiting and spending time in Kildare, It was always lovely to be there and visit the cousins and family. One of the locals was a man named Jim that was an ex of her mothers and he would be in the pub having a drink with his friends and always acknowledged them when they were there. It didn't take long for him to be having a drink with her mother and obviously something was being generated again between them both. There was a much younger friend of his by the name of Pj who would always make his way to her to chat to her regardless of if Paul was with her or not. He was lovely, A tall, handsome, funny man with such a gentle way about him. Her Grandad was very fond of him and would be quite happy to see them together. If he had her Grandad's approval he must be a nice man. He was so easy to talk to, so easy to be in his company and he made her laugh out loud with his stories and jokes, She was attracted to him, to his ways, to his character and personallity and kindness, and he was very handsome. But of course she wasn't looking for anyone as she had Paul so that was that. Her mother had rekindled a romance with an old boyfriend of hers called James from her teenage years when she was growing up in Kildare so now there was an extra reason for the mother to visit home in Kildare. James would now travel to Clare to see Mary and then he started bringing Pj with him for the company. They would arrive and she was always glad to see Pj and was still living with Paul but Pj was always nice and kind to her and she really liked that. Paul was returning to his old ways, She was never sure when he would leave and never sure when he would return, She couldn't continue like this, She had a little baba that would ask "where daddy" and that would break her heart everytime, enough was enough and she finally told him to go and landed anything that was belonging to him down to his brothers house, She had to make the break for her own sake and the sake of her little man Steven, It was 1998 and something had to give. The trips were more frequent now as her Grandad had was getting older and frailer as the years caught up with him. Her once strong, healthy grandad was deteriorating all the time and time with him was more precious now. The more frequent trips meant that she would see Pj when she was in Kildare, She had told him that Paul and her had split up and they just carried on as before, having a drink, a chat and a laugh, it was so nice and comfortable to be around him. Paul had been gone since May and the season was coming to an end so then they were freer to make more trips to Kildare. On the 22nd of November 1998 she had her first kiss with Pj. They had gone for a drink in the local pub and then onto Nass to a nightclub but they couldn't get in because her younger cousin was with them and had no id with her so they were turned away, so they were heading back to her aunts house, where Steven would stay when in Kildare and dropped off her cousin and she stayed in the car to say goodnight to Pj and they had their first kiss. It was magical, the butterflies in the tummy, the swooning, it all happened, it was fabulous. They said goodnight and they made plans to meet the next day with

Steven and go somewhere together. This became the routine when in Kildare, Pj would always go out with her and take her and Steven on days out the following days. It didn't take very long for Steven to be very happy in Pj's company and holding his hand. Steven and her were really liking the reliability and care and kindness that was being given to them by Pj, It was so different to be so well treated and thought of. Their romance involved a lot of travel for the 2 of them between Clare and Kildare. Pj would travel down to Clare, and she would travel up with her mother and Steven in the car or sometimes for weekends on the bus with Steven. It was lovely when it was just the 3 of them, they always returned with a very tired little boy who would have had the best day ever with Pj and his Mammy. Everything was going great between them, Pj had bought her a mobile phone so they could talk when ever they wanted and of course Steven would hog the phone for a chat as well. Things were going very well but her mother was not best pleased with it and would try and plant doubts about Pj being unfaithful to her and the mother was in contact with Paul and would invite him to call to the house to visit Steven, She would try anything to disturb and soil what was going on between her and Pj, but now matter what obstacle the mother put down they always came out the better of it. The mother had liked Pj at the start but she wasn't comfortable with him now as there was a real chance that her daughter had a chance at happiness and that did not sit easy with her mother. God forbid the mother would lose control of her daughter to such a nice caring man. Into the year 2000 her Grandad was getting alot more treatment and doctors visits and hospital stays but he always made it back home, but in 2001 her lovely Grandad had been diagnosed with cancer and had to go to hospital for treatment. It devastated her that her beautiful Grandad was sick and in hospital and she prayed hard that he would recover and be ok. Her Grandad had his operation but he was then moved to a nursing home in Athy as there was no one at home in his house that would be able to provide full time care for him. She went to see him in the nursing home and her grandad begged and pleaded with her to take him out of there and bring him home, she could bring him home to his house but her granny would not have been able to take the care of him that was needed. Grandad deteriorated fast and only 6 weeks later he died, She thinks he died of a broken heart because he accepted that he had to stay in the nursing home he just gave up. That had a devastating effect on, She felt helpless that she couldn't do more, She was broken hearted and angry that he was gone, and 20 years later, She still thinks of him everyday. Her mother was drinking more now that her father had passed and it gave her the reason to drink everyday. It was getting harder to live with the mother as everyday involved drink, shouting and general mayhem in her life. It was becoming harder to cope and just live some sort of a normal quite life. Pj had asked her and Steven to move to Kildare and she said she would in October of that year after the season. One day in September, the busiest month, it just all came to a head and she literally could not take another minute of what was happening. After she had cooked and served the breakfast for the guests and done all the change overs she was finished for the day around 3pm so she had got some of her own laundry and put it in the washing machine only for her mother in a drunken rage to take the clothes out mid cycle and dump them outside the back door. She was angry, upset and totally disgusted with her mothers behaviour with her and her sons laundry. She rang Pj very upset and explained what had happened, Without even blinking an eye he told her to call a taxi and fill it with whatever she needed to get out of there and he would pay the taxi once her and Steven arrived at his home place at whatever time that night. She put whatever she needed into black bags called a taxi and left with maybe 6 large black bags, and 4 boxes of stuff and what ever toys would fit into the taxi and headed to Kildare. It was an exhausting trip and they didn't arrive until around 10pm, but Pj was there to meet and help them and pay the taxi. When they got to Pj both Steven and her were upset and tired but relieved to have escaped their horrible situation and were now safe with Pj. Her and Steven were in the safe refuge of Pj's bedroom in his parents house and it was a home of, Welcome, love and care, it was nothing like she was used to. The phone calls had started from the minute she left from her mother, all sorts of cursing, abuse and threats was flung at her for leaving. He would turn her phone off but when it was on it was hot from all the cals that were coming through. Sometimes Pj would answer the phone and her mother would stall in her rant at her to inform Pj what a useless whore, tramp, no good cunt he had gotten and even told him about her first baby that she had given up for adoption but to her shock Pj already knew and so there was nothing to hurt her and Pj with. Pj was fantastic through all of it, he took on a role of protector and he certainly was their saviour. It didn't take long until Paul, with her mother in the background, started ringing with threats about her and Steven but Pj always handled those bullshit calls, nothing was going to phase him. She had a worry that if they both annoyed Pj enough that Pj would leave her and Steven because no man could stick this mess that happening to him and her and Steven. They lived at Pj's parents house for a month and then rented a mobile and put it in Pj's brother's back garden. It was heaven, It was a 2 bedroom, basic mobile home and it was their home until they could find a place to rent. Of course the calls continued but they were dwindling out as time went by. Steven had started in the local school, and she was working in the local mushroom factory while he was t school, so everyone was settled and happy out, It was going great, She was with the man she loved and she knew for sure that he loved her and Steven and they were happy and content in their bubble and the start of their life together. A year later they found out that she was pregnant and it was the topping on the cake, her and Pj were both delighted with the news and Steven was excited to be getting a sibling. The effort to find a house or apartment revved up a gear with her now being pregnant, and luckily for them they heard about a 3 bedroom house in the local village of Coill Dubh that would be perfect for them. They got the house and were able to move in before Christmas. It was perfect for them, A local school, shops, post office and public buses that travelled to and from Dublin every hour. After that Christmas she transferred Steven to the local school as it was a lot easier for everyone. Her mother had started phone her a while before this and things were a lot calmer and easier as she wasn't drinking too much and had accepted that she was now gone to Kildare and her life was now with Pj, Steven and the new baby that was on the way. Even her father was calling to her house on some occasions and she treated him casually and with a sad content, as she had moved on from all that mess and was trying to hardest just to live and be happy. Not long until April arrived and she was due on the 8th of April but no sign of the boy she thought she was expecting. An appointment was made for her to be induced on the 17th of April and hopefully the baby would come sooner as she really was anxious and ready for this baby to be here. Her and Pj arrived early that morning at Mullingar hospital and were checked in and it was show time all of a sudden, she was hooked up to a drip and she was given something to start her labour. It was a very long day with only mild pain and nothing else really going on, She spent a lot of time walking the ward with Pj to try and encourage the baby to make progress out. It was heading for night time and Pj was told to come back in the morning as nothing was going to happen that night. They were both tired and disappointed as they thought the baby would be there by that night. Pj arrived back that morning and they were both ready for the baby to arrive, the doctor told them that no matter what the baby was coming today, which just so happened to be the Good Friday of the Easter weekend. It was all go from the early morning, She was given something in a drip and that kick started a stronger pain and labour. Her waters were broke later for her to speed up her labour but they discovered that the baby might be in a little bother and stressed because the colour of the waters indicated a problem and things really kicked in from there. The labour pains were crippling and she wasn't coping well as she was now in intense pain and struggling as she was so tired. She was given an epidural and it was magic. Her and Pj were not too concerned as everything seemed under control and things were progressing nicely, Her contractions were not as intense with the epidural so she was able to nap in between the contractions. It was now heading for night time again and wasn't in any hurry to come out. The midwife checked her after a while and all of a sudden it was a mild panic. She was told to now start pushing with all her might as they needed the baby out now as it was stressed and needed delivering straight away. It had gone from being calm to now having a Doctor standing at the end of her bed waiting with a tube to insert into the babies airway for it to breathe as soon as its head was delivered. It got very frightening very quickly but she held onto Pj and gave it her all and shortly after that a baby was born,

The doctor was working on its airway only its head out while she was still pushing down to get the rest of the baby out. It was delivered and the announcement was that they had a baby girl. She was convinced that there was a mistake as she honestly thought that she was having a boy for the previous 6 months while pregnant. But while she was trying to digest that news there was an overwhelming fear in her, Her baby was surrounded by 2 midwives, and a doctor and no noise, or cry being heard from that little baby. Not a word was spoken, just a long, anxious wait for some noise from that little girl, finally after what seemed like an eternity there was an almighty bawl and cry to which she nearly passed out from relief that her baby was ok and shock that she now had a daughter. Pj got to hold her first and he took that little bundle and just breathed her in and she knew instantly that his heart was completely taken by this little lady that was to be called Katie. They got home on Easter Sunday and their new venture started with now 2 children and it was bliss. They had the usual up and downs in life but they were all happy and content. Pj got very sick the next year with his heart and it was a frightening time for all of them. He was only 37 years old and he was suffering from heart damage and high blood pressure and he was in hospital for a month which was turning her upside down with emotion and fear at the thoughts of losing her wonderful Pj. It was frightening for her but she always never got too comfortable in contentment and happiness as she was always expecting something bad to happen when things are going well. Thankfully after some recovery time at home Pj was able to return to work at his business of a taxi driver now that he was getting better. Thankfully there was no major drama occurring around their lives, Steven was settled in the local school, Katie was being such a beautiful and fun toddler, Pj was kept busy with work and totally into his role as Dad, and she was dare she say it, Happy, Secure and in love with her family and her life. The years were going in the blink of an eye. The day came for Katie to start playschool as she was now ready to go and explore, learn and have mighty fun with her little buddies for a few hours for 5 days a week. Katie was so happy to be going to school and over that weekend Katie was extra tired and napping a lot but her mammy put it down to the excitement of starting play school on the Monday and possibly the post trauma of the poor child falling into a bed of nettles a few days previous and an emergency visit to the doctor for all the pain from the stinging Katie got all over her from the said nettles and the extra painkillers they gave the baba for it. Monday morning arrived and Steven was starting a new year in school into 4th class and Katie was up since early morning with the excitement of her new venture in playschool. Off they went with big goodbyes from Daddy and there was tears of course but only from Mammy. It was only a 2 and a half hour stint for Katie so when she was picked up she declared she wanted tomorrow to be there already so that she could to back to Nuala her playschool teacher as she was now Katie's new most favoritest person. Katie was in the car and within seconds had fallen asleep on the 5 minute journey home, They put it down to tiredness after her busy morning but something wasn't right as Katie just wanted to sleep the majority of the and had to woken up for meals. An appointment was made for the doctor the following day after playschool just to see what might be going on and maybe just a vitamin was needed for Katie. Off to school again and then pick up Katie at lunch time for her appointment with the doctor. Explained to him the excessive napping and drinking a bit more than usual, very thirsty over the few days. He just looked at mammy and said i need to do a little finger prick test for a drop of blood from Katie as i think i know what is going on, Great at least he knew and would prescribe some medicine and all would be well again in the world. Katie did not appreciate getting her finger pricked by this little device and the for him to take some blood from her finger, She was quite upset with him but too tired to be argumentative with him or mammy. He came back a few minutes later and with a very sincere apology in his voice he said '' I am so sorry but Katie has Diabetes''. He started writing a letter with an urgency about him and he was explaining that Katie will be going to hospital for a few days to get the help needed to work with the Diabetes and everything would be done at the hospital. Mammy didn't have a clue what was going on, All she heard was Diabetes, hospital for a few days because Katie was crying because she would miss some days in playschool, but that was ok and mammy presumed a few days in hospital would treat this Diabetes thing and that would be the end of it. Little did they both know what was ahead of them that day. As she was leaving the doctor gave her the letter for the hospital and told her that it was straight to the hospital as she had a very sick little girl that needed urgent care and not to even stop at home for clothes or anything because it was urgent to get there asap. She did have one stop and that was to pick up Steven who also was like a grump as he was taken out early from school that day. Straight to Tallaght hospital with them. Pj was on his way and would meet them there as Mammy had rang him and told him what to gather up at home for their few days stay at the hospital. They went to the children's emergency department and handed in the letter and within a minute Katie was brought in and put in a cubicle where a doctor and 2 nurses appeared and straight away were putting in lines to hook up iv's and more finger pricking, bloods taken and a very traumatised 3 year old that was scared and just wanted to go home. There was a panic and an urgency to everything and it then dawned on mammy and daddy that there little woman was in a whole lot of bother here. When the panic had settled a little bit the doctor sat with them and explained that Katie had Type 1 Diabetes and that unfortunately that it was a lifelong condition and that Katie would not ever get better from it. Mammy's first thoughts were panic and anger that her baby girl had gotten this terrible and then being so overwhelmed that week with having to learn how to calculate and measure insulin before injecting it into her baby at every mealtime and injecting extra for corrections when her blood sugars are high as well as being ready 24/7 to catch her low blood sugars and treat them. The parents had now become carer's, nurse's, dietician's, nutritionists, experts in counting and measuring crabs and lastly Mum and Dad, Every other title was first in the care of Katie, Keeping her monitored, alive and well was the new normal and it was a frightening, exhausting, worrying, traumatic, heartbreaking and huge responsibility to be handed. No longer a care free nights sleep or a trip in the car, Every hour of the day required planning and care to deal with the new normal in their lives and the whole family gave it their all. There were many visits to the children's clinic to keep monitored and trying to get everything balanced. Both parents were always on alert and Mammy was really struggling 2 years later. It had got to where she was just completely falling apart at the seams with worry and exhaustion trying to make sure that nothing bad would happen her little girl, the pressure of taking such intense care of her girl was breaking her. At one of the clinics one of the Diabetes nurses took her aside and asked how she was coping and she started to cry and the tears just flowed and would not stop, they both sat there while Mammy was given the time and space to recover from falling apart in that moment of being asked how she was doing, and the nurse just sitting with her with no judgement just concern, While Katie played in the playroom with one of the hospital team. It was suggested to her that she could attend some counselling and talk to someone, it would only be for six one hour weekly sessions and it might help her. She decided to give it a go and maybe she might not be so anxious and worried. Off she went for her first appointment and she had a lovely counsellor. She was very easy to talk to and in all her years of breaking down when speaking about her childhood and crying when telling the details it was somehow easier to tell her as she just let her talk with no interruption or judgement but encouraged her to tell her story, even the parts where she was ashamed of, like the abuse and bringing it on herself and for being such a horrible, troublesome child, for making her parents so mad at her and having to be dealt with and then apologising for being so overprotective of her own children and making sure that nothing bad would happen to them in her care or on her watch. But now the issue was that she had become so enthralled in the worry and anxiety of being the very best protector that she was struggling in every aspect of her life. It was slowly killing her this realisation that she was not loved or protected by her parents. Her and Pj as parents were there to love, protect, care , nurture and raise their children the very best way that they could but in her realisation that this is how it is supposed to be it gave her the insight that she was not loved, protected or cared for by the so called parents that she had the worse curse ever to be handed. There was a sadness that took over her and 3 sessions into her counselling it was arranged that she would have a weekly hour with a specialist childhood sexual abuse counsellor. Where did this come from she was thinking as she wasn't sexually abused by anyone as no sex had taken place but in the experts minds they thought and felt that it was an abuse of a horrendous nature and sexual content to it that was never dealt with by her as she had always been tuned and reminded all her life how it was her fault and what a terrible burden she was to them and everyone around her. Her new, more in-depth counselling started and it was uncomfortable to relay such details and accounts of her early life from the beginning as with every detail she somehow felt like she was re-living the episodes and often left that office physically sore and drained after recounting such details and visions from her past. Unbeknown to her at the time she was now starting a journey of healing and a journey of forgiven herself for feeling such hate and disgust towards herself for being the disgusting child that she was and the horrendous teenager and the adult woman with all her dirty secrets, She had to be literally re-tuned to a better way of thinking of herself, a different way of looking at herself and a way to see the beauty and innocence that was taken and dragged away from her by ill minded monsters and learn how to love the woman that she now was, which still she didn't think deserved love , care or respect. It took a lot of work over those 6 months for her to realise that that she had been sexually abused for their purposes, the very fact that she was stripped naked and tied up while being beaten had the sexual element to it as was the sexual abuse by that other man for his pleasure, the nearly everyday abuse by random hitting, shouting, pushing, demining name calling and reminders of how little she mattered and how fat and disgusting she was but her fat had sometimes made her feel protected, She at least felt if people looked at her with disapproval it was because of her size and not the shame that they might see she was hiding. After the toughest six months of re-tuning her mind and learning to love and care for her a lot better she starting focusing on all that is good and great about her and grieving for that small girl that lived in hell for the majority of her younger life it turns out she is a very nice woman, a great Mum, a loving wife, that does the very best that she can to fit in and enjoy life and hopefully keep everyone in her care safe and well. One of the major things that came to life in her counselling was her unresolved heartbreak around her adopted baby boy Patrick. He had been on her mind a lot, She was always feeling guilty and lost that he had to be adopted and that she felt like she had no other choice in the world at that time. Over the years she had received many updates and photos from his parents and she now had a yearning to meet him. She did enquire into it but the new social worker told her that he would not be told of any desire to meet him until he would reach 21 years old. A couple of months before he would turn 21 she did enquire again from the social worker about a meeting now that he was nearly 21. He was told that she would like to meet him and he was happy to meet her too. She cried for two days with the happiness of getting to see him in person, she cried with the excitement, the anticipation, the nerves, the what if's, the biggest what if being that does he only want to meet her to tell her how useless she is and to fuck off for herself. Filled with every emotion a time and place was set for the meeting, It was to take place at a hotel in Athlone and the social worker told her to bring a friend for support for after the meeting. Even though it was only a few weeks until the meeting she was getting more and more excited with everyday that passed. Finally the day had arrived, She hadn't slept a wink with the nervousness that had taken over her. She was up early, too nauseous to eat, too excited to sit and drink tea, and finally off she went with her friend for the 2 hour journey to Athlone. They arrived at the car park and just as she was getting her car park ticket at the entrance barrier Patrick walked straight in front of the path of the car as he was heading for the front door and she caught her first glance of him in person. She immediately started to shake and found it very difficult to concentrate on parking the car or even speak as she was somehow frozen in herself and was not functioning properly or coherently. A few deep breaths and lots of encouragement from her friend got her calm and collected to go in and see him. She was met and welcomed by the social worker and was told that he was waiting for on the veranda outside and tea had been ordered for them both. The social worker told her friend to come back in an hour that is was just going to be him and her together for the hour and then they would be joined by the people we brought with us. Deep breaths, Wipe the tears, Try and stop shaking, It was time to step out and say Hello, The social worker walked her to the door and she caught sight of him again and her legs would not work at taking the steps onto the veranda. She thought she was going to faint, An almighty feeling greater than she had ever experienced had frozen her to stop where she stood. The social worker took her by the hand and it somehow released her from the hold and she walked towards him and he was coming towards her and in that moment she felt like she had that baby boy back. They both reached out and she really hugged him and he returned the same wonderful hug. She did cry, She cried because she knew in that moment that he wanted to see her and not for any reason to give out to her or tell her to fuck off. They started talking about everything that was going on in their lives, He was going to college, He had a steady girlfriend, that he had brought along on the day, He had the most wonderful parents and spoke of them with great love and honour, He had a brother and 2 sisters, a wonderful balanced life of college, family and lots of travel all over the world. He was just so lovely, mannerly, considerate, handsome and what struck her was how easy the conversation was with the two of them, honestly like they had been great friends all their lives and the talk just flowed so easily. They talked about everything current and looked over old photos from over the years that she had been sent by his parents. All too soon the social worker joined them at the table, she had been sitting in the hotel keeping an eye on them and how things were going. She was happy that everything went so well and she was making a plan of how to communicate from here and make arrangements for future meetings. He would be 21 in 3 weeks and he was happy for her to travel to Sligo to see him during the week of his 21st birthday. She was delighted that she would get to see him so soon again and that there was a definite plan in action. Her friend and his girlfriend joined them soon after to say hello for a few minutes. It really could not have gone much better. She honestly felt like a bit of her heart that had been aching for years was finally healed. She felt like a burden had left her and she travelled home to Kildare that day so happy and content to have finally seen him and to know how great he was with everything in his life. She arrived home to a wonderful man Pj that gave her another great hug and listened to her as she spoke excitedly about her meeting and how lovely he was and all about her plans for future meetings and how much she was looking forward to getting to know him and explaining everything that he would need to know eventually. Her boy at home Steven was curious as to how it went also, He knew about Baby Patrick and that she was gone to meet him as an adult and he was happy that she was getting to see him. He asked lots of questions about and was hoping that he too might get to meet him in ime. And of course he would as would Katie and Pj, but for now it was just going to be him and her and that was perfect. She travelled to Sligo three weeks later for a birthday lunch and to give him a present. The social worker had warned her just to give a gesture gift, Nothing to big or expensive, So it was a gift of motorcycle gloves to keep his hands warm when he was on his scooter. She had a lovely day, Lunch in Strandhill and then back to his apartment that he shared with his girlfriend in Sligo. They got talking and she informed him about his biological dad and how it never would have been an option for her to be with him and how it was not possible to keep him in the circumstances she was in at the time and without delving too far into it he took what he needed from it and left it there for another day. Everytime she would see him she would give a bit more of her story and he always listened and understood and never judged her for any of it. Things were going great and smoothly with them and it was a great healing for her to have him in her life. She was now turning 40 in January and really felt in a great place to give up her smoking habit of 40 cigarettes a day, which after 27 years a smoker was no easy task. But she had a huge bit of wonderful news and everything in her life was coming together. Herself and Pj had decided that they would get married that year and so a small wedding in the local church and a party in the local pub was arranged. 2012 was going to be the year that everything finally slotted into place and her heart was filled with love and pride and her family by her side. Her and Pj are a very relaxed couple and so a no fuss wedding was organised which consisted of a small church wedding followed by a party in the local pub with food and music and hopefully lots of fun for everyone. It was now time for Pj, Steven and Katie to meet Patrick and hopefully get on with and accommodate each other in her blended family. They agreed to meet for bowling, She arrived with her gang who she had warned to be nice to Patrick and he arrived with his girlfriend, She need not have worried as Patrick, Steven and Katie and Pj all jelled straight away and the bowling was the perfect activity for this meeting. There was a lot more pressure on Patrick as he was meeting Steven and Katie who were 7 and 14 years in difference of age to him and he had to adjust to them both where as Steven and Katie had each other to lean on. She was filled with joy that her 3 children could just flow with each other as well as Patrick girlfriend and her Pj, there was even some rivalry with the bowling which added great fun to the day. It was a wonderful day and a forever treasured memory and went so well. Her wedding to Pj was set for 02/08/2012 and was fast approaching, Patrick and his girlfriend were also going to be there, The joy alone of getting married to the forever true love of her life was wonderful but to have her 3 children there was the ultimate gift for her. She was wearing a wedding dress, which was a surprise as she did say that a dress was never on her mind but she had spotted one and tried it on and it was meant to be. Her son Steven walked her up the aisle, Her son Patrick walked her bridesmaid up the aisle and her daughter Katie danced up the aisle to Bruno Mars belting out "I think i want to marry you" on a stereo in the church. It was an emotional day for her, No Mother or Father to watch her with pride getting married, but if they had been there they would have destroyed it for her, No little sister there either as the parents had divided their relationship with hate and destruction and their malice had pulled them apart, but she had Pj, Patrick, Steven and Katie and she was the happiest she had even been, Getting married to the true love of her life with their children looking on. They had the most beautiful, intimate wedding with just some family and friends in the church on a glorious afternoon. Everything went beautifully, They were having a party in the local pub for 120 guests with music, food and fun to be had by all. It was day filled love, excitement, joy, wonder, laughter, happiness, fun, pride, music and song followed by 2 weeks on Achill Island wit the kids and the dog. It was a new start for her as she now had a new last name and that gave her another little release from her past and it gave her a new strength. Life continued as normal as it could be but she made the decision that there would be no ore contact with either of her parents. Her mother was back drinking heavily and living in Lisdoonvarna and her father was living with her in the big house and it was time to stop letting them abuse her with phone calls that only contained name calling and threats to her. She had enough of it and by letting them into her life she was facilitating the horrible treatment that they were bestowing on her. Time to break free and live. Her first and finally steps were to ignore all phone calls from both parents and it was working a treat until it went beyond reason with up to 40 or 50 calls a day as well as messages being left. She was at breaking point and made an appointment to speak to a Garda in Ennistymon to make a statement about all her years of abuse as a child and of what was now happening. She travelled to Lisdoonvarna with a new determination and grit that she had to stop them and just wanted peace in her life. Her appointment was with a lovely Garda that listened to her and wrote every detail and he was all too familiar with Peter and Mary as they kept the local Garda very busy with their fighting and arguing on a regular basis. He explained that if she wanted to proceed with a court hearing that she had to prove that it happened and that they were presumed innocent until proven guilty. She felt let down immediately as she had to fight for a justice for that little lost girl and even now she couldn't help her as she wasn't feeling as strong if she had to fight so hard to get justice while they were deemed innocent until a final verdict. She needed a guarantee because to relive every detail and no justice at the end would finally break her and the chance of her not handling was a risk she could not take as her own children and husband were her happiness and she needed to protect herself from anything destroying her and her life. She made the decision not to pursue it but she did want them confronted with it and so the Garda did visit them and tell them all that he now knew and unless they wanted to end up in prison he would advice them to leave her be and no further contact, It worked and finally she had no contact from her father but her mother still rings and is diverted to message minder with her pleas for her daughter to just cop on and speak to her with the illusion that her mother deserves better after all that she done for her through her life as a child and adult, obviously the fantasy that she was a caring and good mother is still with her, other times she will ring the message minder and her true colours appear again with the name calling and threats which no longer bother or upset her daughter. August 2015 she was contacted to be told that Paul, the dad of her son Steven was in a coma in Limerick hospital. She hadn't had any contact with him since she left Lisdoonvarna as Paul had no interest in a continuing relationship or visits with Steven, Thankfully Steven had Pj as his father to nurture and care for him and he is his father in every way. She wasn't sure what to do about the situation but she told Steven and he had no feelings about it as he didn't know Paul and only had vague memories of him. They decided not to go to see him as he was part of their lives anymore and he had plenty of family around him for support when he would come out of his illness. He made a recover of sorts, He did not get back to full health and was very ill after that time. His niece contacted her again and said that Paul would like to meet up with her and Steven if it was possible as his health was bad. She was given his phone number and when she and Steven were ready they rang him to make arrangements about meeting up. He couldn't travel as he was hooked to an oxygen tank 24 hours a day so it was decided that her and Steven would travel to him. They left early from Kildare to Ennis and went to his house, Neither of them realised how ill Paul was until they saw him. He was using a walker, he hadn't much power in his legs and he was connected to oxygen all the time. He was extremely nervous about meeting Steven as he was still outside smoking a cigarette while she went ahead in. He had last seen Steven as a 5 year old boy and now a 19 year old man was about to come into the house. The usual niceties were spoken and she was struck by how much this one time strong, well built, charming man had failed so much in health at the age of 54. The meeting went well and everyone got on just fine and these visits continued every 3 or 4 months and each time there was chat, laughter and best wishes when saying Goodbye. It was going well with them for the next 2 years and they had settled into regular meetings and the 3 of them getting on great, but Paul's health deteriorating every time they had a visit. They had visited for Steven's 21st birthday and Paul was very unsteady on his feet but was doing his best to hide it and cover up how much he had gone downhill with his illness. They said their Goodbyes and made plans to catch up again at the end of July. Paul rang her on the 19 of July to tell her he was back in hospital but he was in good spirits. He said he had another chest infection and was admitted for a few days and was hoping ton be home for Steven's visit which was to be the following week. That was the last time she got to speak to Paul, She received a phone call on Friday evening from Paul's niece to say that he had taken a turn for the worst and he only had hours to live. What the hell was happening, This couldn't be real, It wasn't registering with her as a real situation. She rang the hospital straight away and was put through to a nurse on his ward that indeed did say that it was only a matter of hours before Paul would die. What a nightmare to be facing, She got Steven straight away and explained the urgency to get to Limerick Hospital to say Goodbye. They left home in Kildare with an urgency to get there to try and make it before he wasn't able to hold on any longer. They arrived at 9.15pm and were frightened to see Paul struggling to breath. She wasn't sure if he knew if they were there but the nurse assured her that he knew they were in the room. His two sisters and brother were there also as well as some niece's and nephew's whom she hadn't seen in years. They gave them their space to say Goodbye to him and within 20 minute's of arriving to him he passed. It was so sad that he was gone with no warning or preparation. They knew he was very ill but her and Steven thought that maybe he would be around for another 2 years at least. They returned to Kildare that night, Exhausted and bewildered as to what had just happened that night. They of course got themselves together, sorted and returned to Clare for the next few days for the funeral and it was sad that after 2 years of having back him in their lives and getting to know them that he now was gone and laid to rest at such a young age.

Lots of things have happened to her since, She has had plenty of ups and downs but no matter what she has her wonderful husband and saviour Pj by her side and her children that are turning into bold, strong, hard working and fearless adults who are ready to take on the world. She lives with a pride and a forever unbreakable love in her heart for her Pj and her children. Her mother is living in

Lisdoonvarna in the big red house and drinking herself into oblivion every single day while her father is living there also with his mind working overtime putting on a show of being a great man but there are exactly where they deserve to be, Together yet lonely and just wasting the days until their ending. She doesn't wish them anything, She just wants peace and quite, and wants no contact or meeting with them but she just might face them one day and tell them that they haven't destroyed her will and want to live. She now has a great relationship with her sister Marie after many missed years, The secret to that is to not even talk about our parents and we will be fine and hopefully nothing will part us again.

Finally she is in a place that she never thought she would survive to get to. She is a 47 year old woman who feels quite young at heart but in body is crippled from abuse and beatings and in chronic pain every day and night but it is a reminder that she is here and doing great no matter how hard they tried to darken her light and destroy her soul, Something in her kept her going and even though she thought that child was weak it turns out that child was fighting for her life and as a woman has now won the fight and conquered the monsters and hopefully saved the child within herself. As a child she had begged God to take her sometimes when the pain was so bad she thought she was dying, She thought someday's that she was going to be killed, She had days that she wanted to take herself out of the world, She remembers nothing but brutality and sadness for that little girl, and then shame for the older child and the disgust, condemnation around the pregnant teenager, and the dirty secrets that the now woman had about her adopted baby.

Today she has no shame, no disgust, no fear and no apologies for writing this, Because she finally has a name, and she is happy in her her body, mind and soul and nobody can destroy her ever again,

And finally her name,

Her name is CAROLINE.

Printed in Great Britain
by Amazon